MW00477655

An Introduction to

SOUTHERN CALIFORNIA

Butterflies

FRED HEATH

Photographs by
HERBERT CLARKE

Mountain Press Publishing Company
Missoula, Montana
2004

FRONT COVER PHOTO:
'Desert' Black Swallowtail (*Papilio polyxenes coloro*)

BACK COVER PHOTOS:
Spring White (*Pontia sisymbrii*), Gulf Fritillary (*Agraulis vanillae*),
and Bramble Hairstreak (*Callophrys dumetorum*)

Library of Congress Cataloging-in-Publication Data

Heath, Fred, 1943–
    An introduction to southern California butterflies / Fred
Heath ; photographs by Herbert Clarke.
        p. cm.
Includes bibliographical references and index.
    ISBN 0-87842-475-X (pbk. : alk. paper)
    1. Butterflies—California, Southern.   I. Clarke, Herbert, 1927–
II. Title.
    QL551.C3H43 2003
        595.7'89'097949—dc22

                                                2003017939

PRINTED IN HONG KONG BY MANTEC PRODUCTION COMPANY

MOUNTAIN PRESS PUBLISHING COMPANY
P.O. Box 2399 • Missoula, Montana 59806
406-728-1900

To my daughter Holly, who shares my enchantment with butterflies.
—FRED HEATH

To Olga—I am grateful for more than 50 wonderful years!
—HERBERT CLARKE

Overwintering Monarchs, Ellwood, California

TABLE OF CONTENTS

ACKNOWLEDGMENTS

Many people have contributed to the production of this book. Their encouragement, suggestions, and companionship have greatly added to the enjoyment of our working together in creating a publication that we hope will help introduce many newcomers to the fascinating world of butterflies.

Kimball Garrett sparked our initial interest in butterflies, while over the years our longtime friends, Pam and Larry Sansone, encouraged us to take flower and plant pictures. Their enthusiasm and knowledge of botany made for many pleasant hours in the field. Jonathan Alderfer, an outstanding bird artist, graciously drew and revised the map. Tom Frillman patiently guided us through the jungle of computer technology.

We want to especially acknowledge the contribution of Julian P. Donahue who completely and carefully reviewed the text and photographs. His many corrections and suggestions made this a better book.

Olga Clarke took many of the food plant photographs in this book, and if this were not enough, she consistently kept us well fed all through the rigors of work in the field and time spent in front of the computer.

Our grateful thanks to all.

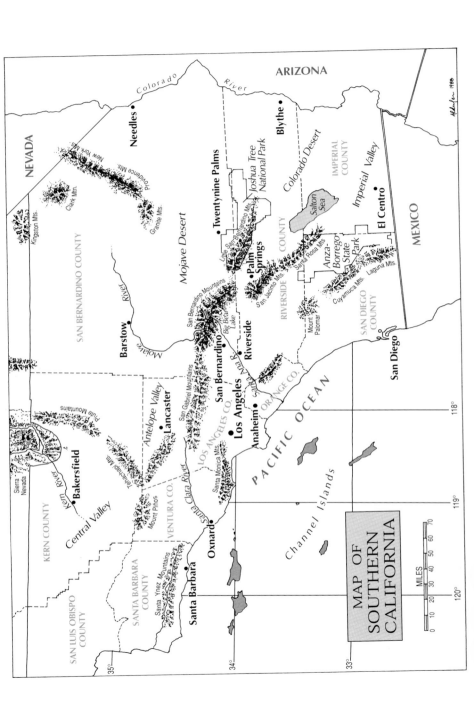

MAP OF SOUTHERN CALIFORNIA

INTRODUCTION

The Purpose of This Book

Butterflies are the poster children of the insect world. They suggest warm, sunny days filled with beautiful flowers. Today a large and growing interest in anything to do with butterflies appears in such diverse areas as jewelry, clothing, live butterfly releases at weddings, advertisements, festivals, home butterfly gardens, and specialty tours and field trips. In addition, many museums, zoos, and private organizations have opened walk-through butterfly gardens with free-flying butterflies imported from all over the world.

You may just want to know the names of some of the local butterflies. This book will certainly enable you to identify the butterflies commonly encountered in Southern California, whether you find them in your home garden or alongside the trail while hiking in our area parks or forests. Along with appreciating their beauty—captured in the photographs in this book—we hope you will also learn a little something about these fascinating insects and begin to understand how they fit into the natural environment and what their various strategies for survival are. This book, as the title indicates, is only an introduction to butterflies. If you are interested in more in-depth information, the books, museums, and Web sites listed under Suggested Resources can help open the door further on the world of these amazing creatures.

What Is a Butterfly?

Classification

Scientists have developed a classification system that encompasses all living things: kingdom is the broadest category; from there we work down to the individual levels of species and subspecies. Butterflies are, of course, in the Animal Kingdom. More specifically, they belong in the phylum Arthropoda (invertebrates with jointed appendages and an exoskeleton) and in the class Insecta (insects). Although most people don't think of them as insects, butterflies have the same basic structure as cockroaches, beetles, and ants: a three-part body, a pair of antennae, and six legs. Within the insect class, butterflies fall into the order Lepidoptera, which includes both butterflies and moths. Lepidoptera means "scale" (*lepis*) "wing" (*ptera*), a reference to the thousands of tiny scales, arranged like shingles on a roof, that make up the wing colors and patterns of butterflies and moths. Scientists who study butterflies and moths are called lepidopterists.

Butterflies versus Moths

Butterflies are differentiated from moths at the next classification level: they are placed in the suborder Rhopalocera, consisting of two superfamilies. Many people wonder about the differences between butterflies and moths. There are several. Generally, butterflies fly during the day, while most moths fly at night. Also, butterflies are usually fairly colorful, while moths are not. The diurnal butterflies tend to use color to distinguish possible mates, whereas the nocturnal moths, since they fly when colors are difficult to see, primarily use scent to find a mate. There are, however, a number of brightly colored moths, some of which fly in the daytime.

One way to distinguish between the two is to look at their antennae: butterflies have clubbed antennae (a wider part at the tip), while most moth antennae are threadlike and tapered to a point at the tip or feathery throughout. Some moths have fat bodies that

White-Lined Sphinx Moth

Day-flying Sheep Moth with nonclubbed antennae

A geometrid moth showing feathery antennae

American Snout Butterfly showing clubbed antennae

may appear furry (the "fur" is actually modified scales). Butterflies fold their wings together above their bodies when resting, while many moths fold their wings alongside their bodies. Finally, moths have a hooklike body part called the frenulum that couples the forewing and hindwing together and makes their flight somewhat stiff compared to that of most butterflies.

Butterfly Families

Butterflies comprise two superfamilies: the Papilionoidea, or true butterflies, and the Hesperioidea, or skippers. Skippers are named for their bouncing flight, which makes them look like they are skipping. They have fat bodies with the head as wide as the thorax and appear quite furry, and many are dull orange or brown; for these reasons people sometimes mistake them for moths. However, skippers have the typical true butterfly's clubbed antennae, generally with a small hook on the end of the club.

Saltbush Sootywing, a skipper, showing hooked antennae clubs

California Giant-Skipper

Butterfly superfamilies are further classified into families. Authorities differ as to how many families there are. The Brushfoot Family (Nymphalidae), which is treated as a single family in this book, is sometimes split into as many as eleven separate families. Using the North American Butterfly Association (NABA) checklist, we have included the five families of true butterflies and one family of skippers found in Southern California in this book. The five true butterfly families are the swallowtails, whites and sulphurs, gossamer-wing butterflies, metalmarks, and brushfooted butterflies.

Parts of a Butterfly

Like all insects, butterflies have six legs, a pair of antennae, and a body that is divided into three parts: the head, with the tongue, eyes, and antennae; the thorax, where the wings, the legs, and the muscles to drive them are attached; and the abdomen, containing the digestive and reproductive organs. Butterflies have two pairs of wings—forewings and hindwings; the forewings are closest to the head. When a butterfly spreads its wings out flat, the surface we see from above is variously referred to as dorsal, uppersides, top, or

Two-tailed Swallowtail below

Forewing

Hindwing

Abdomen

Head

Thorax

above. When a butterfly closes its wings, holding them together above its body, the visible surface is called ventral, undersides, bottom, or below. In this book, we will use the words *above* and *below* to describe these surfaces.

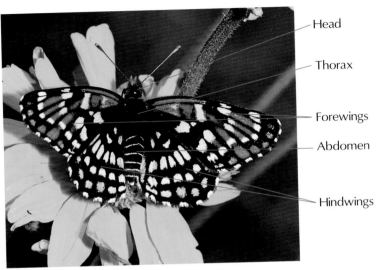

Head

Thorax

Forewings

Abdomen

Hindwings

Leanira Checkerspot (dark form) above

Pine White showing partially coiled proboscis

Proboscis

Butterflies exercise their sense of smell using chemical receptors in the many minute holes in their antennae. This sense enables them to find food plants, seek mates, and recognize rivals. Butterflies use sensory equipment on their feet to taste what they land on. The sense of taste helps the females confirm their food plants for egg laying. Butterfly eyes are compound: they have many facets, each with its own lens and optic nerve. Though they don't transmit a clear image to the butterfly's brain, the eyes are excellent for detecting motion and seeing colors into the ultraviolet range. An adult butterfly drinks flower nectar and other liquids through its tongue-like proboscis. The proboscis is hollow and can draw liquid up just like a straw. When the proboscis is not in use, it is coiled up like a child's party whistle.

The Name Butterfly

Although we can't be sure, butterflies were probably named after a large, bright yellow species called a Brimstone, common in England. This butterfly is particularly abundant in the early spring, at the same time that new mother cows' milk comes in for butter making; thus the connection between butter and these flying, butter-colored insects. Alternatively, some people believe that *butterfly* is a corruption of the word *flutterby*, used early on to describe their flight.

Life Cycle

Like many other insects, such as beetles, flies, ants, and bees, butterflies go through a drastic change in form during their life cycle. This process is referred to as complete metamorphosis. That a worm-like caterpillar can transform into a free-flying butterfly seems nothing short of astounding!

Egg

Butterflies usually lay their tiny eggs directly on the food plant that will sustain the caterpillars when they hatch. The butterfly generally lays the eggs on the plant's leaves or flowers. Some species, such as the fritillaries, lay their eggs on the ground in close proximity to the food plant. Butterfly females actually taste the food plant first with receptors on their feet.

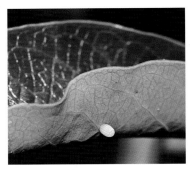

Gulf Fritillary egg

Depending on the species, the female will lay tens to many hundreds of fertilized eggs; she can lay any number from one egg per plant to large masses of eggs together. Normally, eggs hatch in five to ten days, but for species that spend the winter (this is called *overwintering*) in the egg phase, this time can extend to six months or so. The shape of the egg also depends on the species: it can be spherical, spindle-shaped, round and flat, or conical; and it can be smooth, ridged, or covered with other intricate, raised patterns.

Caterpillar (Larva)

The caterpillar or larval stage of the butterfly's life cycle is the eating and growing phase. Whenever you hear a reference to the butterfly's food plant or host plant, it means the plant the caterpillar eats. Depending on the species, caterpillars will eat the leaves, flowers, or new tender shoots of its food plant. Some butterfly species have specific food plant requirements and only use one species of plant or several closely related plants, while others can use plants from many different families. The latter species are usually more common and widespread.

Immediately after the caterpillar hatches from the egg, it starts to eat and grow, usually consuming the eggshell as its first meal. The growing caterpillar soon becomes too large for its outer skin, so it molts, or sheds the old skin. The new skin underneath is looser and allows the caterpillar to continue to grow until this skin in turn becomes too small. Caterpillars molt four to six times; each stage is called an instar. The caterpillar can change color and skin pattern at each instar. Unless the butterfly is going to overwinter as a caterpillar, the caterpillar takes about two to four weeks to grow to full size before it enters the pupal stage.

Gulf Fritillary caterpillar

Pupa (Chrysalis)

During the pupal stage, the butterfly goes through its most remarkable metamorphosis, or form change. The pupa of a true butterfly is often called a chrysalis. As it encloses itself in this hard, lifeless-seeming case, the caterpillar uses silk it excretes to attach the case to a twig, a blade of grass, or another surface; or it hides itself in leaf litter or loose soil. Many of the pupae of skippers (and those of almost all moths) are encased in a cocoon the caterpillar makes from its silken threads. The pupa of the Gulf Fritillary resembles a curled-up dead leaf. Although pupae may look dead, they can and do move.

The pupae of giant skippers move up and down in the hollow part of an agave leaf.

Gulf Fritillary pupa

Inside the pupa, the caterpillar can completely change into a butterfly in one to two weeks. Many butterflies overwinter as pupae: these species stay in the pupal stage for many months to almost a year. Some butterfly species may, under poor conditions such as drought, continue on as pupae for more than a year.

Adult

When the adult butterfly is fully formed, it finally emerges (the technical term is *ecloses*) from the split pupa. It then pumps fluid through its veins to its wings, forcing the wings to open fully. In a few hours, the wings harden and the butterfly is ready for flight. At this point, the butterfly is finished growing.

As the caterpillar stage was the eating and growing phase, the adult butterfly stage is the reproductive phase. Unlike caterpillars, adult butterflies don't consume solid food; they take nectar, and they do this mainly to get enough energy to search out mates and lay eggs.

One question most people ask about butterflies is how long they live—as an adult, the questioner usually means. The adult life span varies from species to species, but on average, butterflies live for about two weeks. Some of the smaller butterflies and the early spring species may only live for a few days. Others that overwinter (or

Gulf Fritillary emerging

hibernate) as adults can live for half a year or more. Species such as the Monarch may have a midsummer brood that only lives for a few weeks, while overwintering individuals may live six or seven months. Not long after a butterfly mates and, in the case of the female, lays its eggs, it has fulfilled its function, and it dies.

Although all the butterflies of a species are roughly the same size, the females, since they must carry the heavy load of eggs, are larger than the males. Occasionally, an individual butterfly is much smaller than the typical adult. These runts result from caterpillars that couldn't find enough to eat and either skipped an instar or just never reached full size before they pupated.

Overwintering

Most butterfly species have a period in their life cycle when they are not active, generally during the cold winter months. This resting period is technically called diapause. When diapause is observed in the adult, or butterfly, phase, it is sometimes called hibernation. In this book, we use the term overwintering, even though it may not seem strictly correct in all cases. For example, the Silvery Blue, which flies in the spring and pupates in the early summer, spends the rest of that year and early the next (so, more than just the winter) in diapause as a pupa.

Different species overwinter in different life cycle stages. Most butterflies overwinter in the caterpillar or pupal stage, but a few overwinter in the egg stage or as an adult. Because of our mild Southern California winters, a number of Southern California butterflies fly all year round and may not have a real overwintering stage, though they may go into reproductive diapause at a certain phase in their life cycle.

Broods

One complete life cycle from egg to adult butterfly is referred to as a generation or brood. When a particular season is mentioned in conjunction with a brood, that season is when the adults are flying.

Thus the spring brood of the Square-spotted Blue starts to fly in April.

Butterflies can have from one to many broods during a year. In scientific terms, a species may be univoltine or multivoltine. Many butterflies do have a specific number of broods each year. The Behr's Hairstreak has one brood, while the Sara Orangetip has two. But some butterflies that have only one brood in our mountains or further north in colder climates can have two or more broods during the longer season in our lowlands. Also, because of our mild climate in Southern California, a number of species continue to have broods throughout the year. The Cabbage White, Marine Blue, and West Coast Lady are good examples of this. In the desert, copious late summer rains in some years may bring out a fall brood of species such as the California Patch and the Tiny Checkerspot.

Behavior

Mating

Since the main function of the adult butterfly is to mate and lay eggs, males have developed various strategies to find females, including patrolling, perching, and hilltopping. The Western Tiger Swallowtail patrols along a streambed or a tree-lined street where its cottonwood or sycamore food plant grows. Many of our whites and sulphurs seem to be in constant motion, patrolling almost non-stop for a female to mate with.

Many of the hairstreaks and skippers, and some of our larger brushfooted butterflies, use perching. The male sits on a conspicuous perch and flies out to investigate any butterfly that happens by. If it turns out to be a male of the same species, the perching butterfly will try to drive the intruder away. During such a challenge, some male hairstreaks and blues spiral around each other while flying up and sometimes out of sight.

Males of a few species fly to the nearest mountain or hilltop and stake out a territory. There they await unmated females, which instinctively know where to find them. These high spots may be far from the food plant, so the females travel back downslope as soon as they have mated. The Pale Swallowtail and the Desert Orangetip are two species that make extensive use of this mate-finding strategy.

Although butterflies may initially find potential mates visually, searching for particular colors and patterns, most species emit pheromones (sexual scent attractants) that clinch the match. The pheromones are species specific and enable the butterflies to recognize potential mates or rivals. When they've located a potential mate, males of most species display with either wings or body or both, and if the female is receptive the two will mate. The male has special organs at the tip of the abdomen that grasp the female during mating. The pair may be locked together for only a few minutes or as long as several hours depending on the species. Occasionally, a coupled pair can be seen flying together. During mating, the male passes a spermatophore—a packet of sperm and minerals—to the female. Both males and females can mate several times.

Melissa Blue pair mated

El Segundo (Square-spotted) Blue male basking

Basking

Butterflies need to warm their flight muscles before they can fly. On somewhat cool days or in the cooler early morning hours, butterflies bask in the sun to raise their body temperatures. They do this in a number of ways, depending on the species. The most straightforward way is to simply spread their wings wide open and present as much surface area as possible to the sun's warming rays. This may present the butterfly watcher with an opportunity to observe or photograph the butterfly above when it normally perches with its wings closed. This basking strategy is a favorite with the whites and sulphurs and the gossamer-wings (see photo of El Segundo Blue male basking at bottom left).

Other species bask with their wings closed. These butterflies typically lean in such a way that their wing surfaces are perpendicular to the sun's rays to get maximum sunlight energy. Some butterflies bask on the open ground or on a rock surface that has already been warmed by the sun. Because warmth is most important to the thoracic flight muscles, many butterflies have darker wing bases and bodies to absorb the heat better where it is needed.

Nectaring

Butterflies are invariably associated with flowers. Most butterflies spend at least a portion of their day imbibing the nectar found within flowers, using their long proboscis much like a straw. The nectar is rich in sugar, which provides the butterfly with the energy to fly in search of mates. In Southern California, buckwheat, sunflower, mint, mustard, yerba santa, and pea are favorite nectaring plants.

Butterflies and the flowering plants that provide nectar have a symbiotic (mutually beneficial) relationship. As a butterfly nectars at a flower, it picks up pollen on its legs and body; it then transfers the pollen to another flower of the same species as it continues to seek nectar. Many of these flowering plants and butterflies (as well as other insects) have coevolved. For example, research has shown that moths with a long proboscis generally specialize in long tubular flowers where the nectar is hidden deep within.

Puddling

Besides the sugars in nectar, butterflies require nutrients such as salt, nitrogen, and amino acids. Since the caterpillars eat plants with few salts and little nitrogen, the butterflies must make up the deficit.

Generally, the males do their part by taking up salts and other necessary nutrients at puddle edges or on wet ground. Sometimes large numbers of butterflies gather at a particularly attractive damp spot, forming "puddle parties" (see photos on pages 66, 73, and 175). The spermatophore that the male passes to the female during mating includes salts and other nutrients she needs along with the sperm.

Many butterflies also get these nutrients from sources such as tree sap, rotting fruit, carrion, urine, and feces. Some butterflies, especially those in the brushfooted family, occasionally land on people to drink their sweat. Butterflies need the nutrients gathered during these behaviors for survival; additionally, they use some of the chemicals for making pheromones.

Population Fluctuations

Many species of butterflies can lay hundreds of eggs, which makes them, like most insects, capable of rapid population surges if environmental conditions are conducive. Heavy winter rains—such as those during El Niño years—can lead to lush vegetation, and thus increased availability of food plants as well as copious nectar sources. Many species of Southern California butterflies are abundant in the spring and summer following a wet winter. The very next year, under drier conditions, some of these same species can be difficult to find at all. The California Tortoiseshell and the Painted Lady are two local species known for their large population swings. In some years, summer thunderstorms in the desert encourage an additional fall brood of some species such as the Juniper Hairstreak, the California Patch, or the Tiny Checkerspot. Then several years might pass before we see these same species in the fall.

Emigration/Migration

Although most of our local butterflies are somewhat sedentary, some species travel long distances during mass emigrations. In years when conditions are excellent, the Painted Lady population in nearby Mexico soars, and in the late winter and early spring, millions of these butterflies emigrate from the south to our area. On some days during these flights, Painted Ladies can literally stop traffic, especially at our desert edges, covering windshields and headlights, clogging radiators, and making the roads slippery. Some Painted Ladies continue north as far as southern Canada.

The California Tortoiseshell, normally a scarce butterfly of our mountain chaparral, has large population surges on occasion, followed by mass emigrations downslope to our lowlands. In exceptional years, a few individuals have even been seen out in the desert.

The mass emigrations caused by population explosions are different from the well-known bidirectional migration of the Monarch. Like birds, Monarchs head north in the spring and return south in the fall. However, unlike birds where the same individuals make the return trip, the southbound Monarchs are several generations removed from the butterflies that made the spring trip north.

Colors and Scales

The striking colors and patterns that endear butterflies to us are made up of many tiny overlapping scales. If you've ever handled a butterfly and afterwards found a colored powdery substance on your fingers matching the color of the butterfly, these were scales. Many people have the erroneous impression that butterflies can't fly with their scales removed, but they can. In fact, in the tropics, a group of butterflies known as clearwings have very few scales and thus mostly transparent wings. The ease with which the scales come off may allow a butterfly to escape an occasional spider web or slip out of a bird's beak, leaving only a few scales behind.

Pigments in the scales produce colors, including black, brown, gray, red, orange, yellow, and white. These pigments can come directly from chemicals in the food plant—green coloration can come from chlorophyll—or they can be manufactured by the butterfly as a caterpillar. Gold, silver, iridescent blue, most greens, and purple are generally structural colors; they are created when ridges in the surface of the scales diffract light or air bubbles beneath the surface cause refraction.

Some butterfly scales produce pheromones and thus play a key part in locating and recognizing mates. Butterfly colors also play a large role in mate recognition. A butterfly's ability to see colors in the ultraviolet range allows it to distinguish patterns and colors not visible to the human eye. Some butterfly species, such as the orange and clouded sulphurs, which to us look very similar in natural light, appear quite different from each other under UV light.

Butterfly coloration can also help butterflies avoid predation in various ways: it can serve as camouflage, mimic another less

Gulf Fritillary below showing silver structural colors with orange and brown pigment colors

palatable species, or warn or scare predators away. For instance, the Monarch butterfly's orange and black are aposematic, or warning, colors that it and many other animals—including poison-arrow frogs, ladybugs, and coral snakes—use to tell potential predators that they are toxic.

As mentioned previously, many butterflies have dark wing bases so that solar energy is better absorbed near the flight muscles on the thorax during basking. Some of the early spring white butterflies go further by reflecting the sun's warming rays with their white outer wings towards the darkened body.

In many butterfly species, the males and females look very similar, while in others, they are sexually dimorphic, meaning each sex has a different appearance. Sexual dimorphism is particularly pronounced in many of the skippers. Swallowtail males and females, on the other hand, are virtually identical. Above, male and female gossamer-wing butterflies are distinct, while below they are alike.

Predation

The butterfly is subject to predators at every stage of its life cycle. Ants and spiders eat butterfly eggs and small caterpillars. Larger caterpillars and even pupae face the same predators plus various wasps, ambush bugs, lizards, small mammals, and birds. These prey on the caterpillars directly, while parasitic wasps and flies lay their eggs on or in the caterpillars. After they've hatched, the larvae of these parasites slowly feed on the still-living caterpillar. Sometimes a caterpillar pupates with small parasitic larvae inside its body. The parasite larvae, protected in the hard pupal case, grow to maturity at the butterfly's expense. The emerging adult parasites leave small exit holes in the dead pupa, evidence of what has occurred.

Adult butterflies must run a gauntlet that includes crab and web-weaving spiders, ambush bugs, dragonflies, robber flies, praying mantises, various toads and frogs, lizards, mice, and birds. Often, a praying mantis is found eating only butterflies of a certain species: the wings left over from its previous kills attract more of the same species of butterfly, making the mantis's job easy.

In response to predation, butterflies have developed various defense strategies. Because of the high mortality rate, most butterfly species lay many eggs. In the caterpillar stage, camouflage is often effective, as anyone who has searched for caterpillars knows. The caterpillars of many species—especially the gossamer-wings, such as the blues—blend in very well with their food plant. Other caterpillars use mimicry. Early instars of many of the swallowtails resemble bird droppings, while the later, larger instars sometimes have huge eyespots that give them the appearance of a small snake. The caterpillars of the milkweed-feeding Monarch and Queen butterflies are bright yellow and black; these aposematic, or warning, colors broadcast to potential predators that the milkweed alkaloids have made the caterpillars toxic.

Some caterpillars hide, particularly those of the brushfooted butterflies; they excrete a silk with which they stick together the folded leaves of their food plant to make a shelter. In other cases, caterpillars defend themselves more actively. Swallowtail caterpillars have a forked gland behind their head called an osmeterium;

BUTTERFLY PREDATORS

A small flycatcher eating a moth

An ambush bug with a captured moth

A yellow jacket attacking a Monarch

BUTTERFLY PREDATORS

rned Lark male feeding caterpillars to nestlings

A Sara Orangetip caught in a spider's web

A praying mantis with the remains of its meal: a pile of Bordered Patch wings

when a caterpillar is threatened, its foul-smelling gland pops out and deters many predators. Other caterpillars have protective spines that help keep parasitic wasps and flies away. One of the more interesting defenses against caterpillar predators—practiced extensively by many of the blues—makes use of ant attendants. The caterpillar exudes a sugar-filled honeydew that sustains the ants, while the ants protect the caterpillar against various predators, often carrying the caterpillar into their nest at night.

Although free-flying adult butterflies are not as vulnerable as caterpillars, they still have predators and ways to avoid predation. As with some caterpillars, toxins from the food plant make a number of butterflies unpalatable. Many of the whites feed on mustards, which have toxic and foul-smelling oils. Birds quickly learn that these rather obvious white butterflies do not make a good meal. Among milkweed butterflies, the caterpillars of the Queen and Monarch in our area have already been mentioned as having bright warning colors; the adults also have orange and black aposematic colors that keep birds away. Some other butterflies that are not toxic take advantage of the birds' aversion through mimicry. The Viceroy, which just enters our area along the Colorado River, looks very much like the Queen at first glance, and birds generally avoid it.

Other butterflies use mimicry to camouflage themselves. From above, the brightly colored Red Admiral and the Hoary Comma are hard to miss. However, when they land and close their wings, they resemble dead leaves and tree bark, respectively, and thus blend in with their surroundings.

The hairstreaks, and to a lesser extent the swallowtails, practice another form of mimicry: head-to-tail mimicry. The hairstreaks have hairlike projections on their hindwings that look like antennae and, usually, a nearby dark eyespot surrounded by brighter colors to focus attention on the "eye." The hairstreak completes the mimicry by facing downward and slowly moving its hindwings back and forth. A bird or other predator is then fooled into biting the tail end of the butterfly, and the butterfly can escape with only a piece out of its wing. The swallowtail's tails also resemble antennae and the dark lines on many swallowtail species may direct the predator's eye to that end of the butterfly.

A number of other butterflies, such as the Great Basin Wood-Nymph, have large eyespots on their wings that they flash at an attacking predator. The predator is briefly startled into thinking it is facing a larger animal, giving the butterfly time to escape.

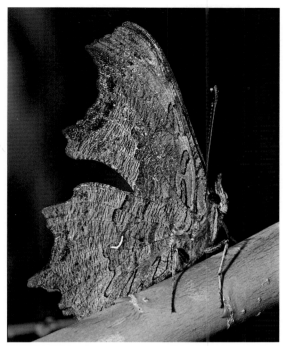

Hoary Comma below looks like tree bark

Red Admiral camouflaged in leaf litter

Gray Hairstreak below showing head-to-tail mimicry with hindwing eyespot and antenna-like tails.

Great Basin Wood-Nymph below flashing eyespot

Scientific versus Common Names

Butterflies, like birds, have two sets of names: scientific names and common, or English, names. The scientific names, most of which are derived from Latin or Greek, allow serious students of butterflies anywhere in the world to know which species is meant. A specific butterfly's scientific name consists of two words that are generally italicized: the first word, always capitalized, is the genus and the second word is the species. For example, the scientific name of the Mourning Cloak is *Nymphalis antiopa*, while the closely related (in the same genus) California Tortoiseshell is named *Nymphalis californica*.

Even these scientific names are not set in concrete and can change as our knowledge of butterfly taxonomy increases. As we better understand the relationships between various species, the species name or even the genus of a butterfly can change. Sometimes it becomes apparent that two very similar-looking butterflies are in fact different species. Conversely, two different-looking butterflies might turn out to be separate subspecies of the same species or just seasonal forms of the same species.

A subspecies is usually defined as a population that is geographically separated from other populations of the same species. Although two populations may look different, they could theoretically interbreed and produce fertile offspring. A butterfly's subspecies adds a third word to the scientific name. The Square-spotted Blue, *Euphilotes battoides*, has an endangered subspecies, the El Segundo Blue: its complete scientific name is *Euphilotes battoides allyni*.

There are still disagreements about—and regular changes made to—scientific names. Until recently, the situation for common names was much worse. Many authors used different common names in different publications. Some authorities believed the common names were not important, as long the scientific names were correct.

Common names don't follow the same rules as scientific names. Several local subspecies have names that make no mention of the commonly accepted species name, as with the El Segundo subspecies of the Square-spotted Blue. The Silvery Blue has common names for both its local subspecies: the widespread Southern Blue and the endangered Palos Verdes Blue—neither name indicates it is a Silvery Blue. Likewise, the Cloudy Copper and the Behr's Metalmark are common names for local subspecies of the Tailed Copper and the Mormon Metalmark, respectively.

To make matters more confusing, the same name is sometimes used to designate two entirely different species. In the Rocky Mountains, for example, the Boisduval's Blue is a very common species of blue butterfly that local butterfliers call the Common Blue. In Arizona, the most common blue is the Spring Azure; it too is called the Common Blue. In 1992, The Lepidopterists' Society published a book by Jacqueline Miller, *The Common Names of North American Butterflies*, that listed twelve common names each for the widespread Pearl Crescent and Mourning Cloak butterflies.

The American Ornithologists' Union (AOU) standardized both the scientific and the English names for birds. Until recently, no such organization existed for butterflies. Some lepidopterist purists felt there was no need for common names. However, the North American Butterfly Association (NABA), formed in 1992, decided that a consistent, standardized list of English names would make the study of butterflies more accessible to the general public. They generated such a list and published it in 1995 as the *Checklist & English Names of North American Butterflies*. The second edition came out in 2001. This publication lists an English and a scientific name for each of the 722 butterfly species found in North America north of Mexico, along with some discussion of the reasoning behind the taxonomy used. The great majority of the butterfly books published in North America since then follow the names in that checklist. This book also uses the NABA names and taxonomy.

Watching Butterflies

Not too many years ago, most butterfly hobbyists enjoyed butterflies mainly through netting and collecting. The wonder of butterfly *watching* was finally extolled by Robert Pyle in his *Handbook for Butterfly Watchers*, first published in 1984. The North American Butterfly Association (NABA) was founded in 1992 "to educate the public about the joys of nonconsumptive, recreational butterflying including listing, gardening, observation, photography, rearing, and conservation." Today, due in part to the efforts of NABA and to the availability of more and more books on butterflies, the number of people going out into the field to watch and identify butterflies is rapidly growing.

Note that while this book does not advocate collecting, we recognize the need for some people to continue collecting butterflies in their efforts to unravel the remaining mysteries of butterfly taxonomy. A better understanding of butterfly relationships can help us define unique species and subspecies and identify their precise ecological requirements; with this knowledge, we can conserve both habitats and butterfly populations.

How to Watch Them

Everyone can enjoy butterflies with the naked eye, but to truly appreciate some of their fine and beautiful markings, you will want to use close-focusing binoculars: ones that can focus down to 5 or 6 feet. Such binoculars will offer you a nice large image of even the smallest butterfly.

Generally, butterflies are most approachable when they are engrossed in taking nectar from a flower, so give the butterfly time to settle. Approach slowly and deliberately—butterflies are excellent at detecting movement. Be aware of your shadow; when it falls across a butterfly, it can sometimes startle the butterfly into flight.

Because butterflies, like most people, emerge in nice weather, it doesn't make sense to look for them unless it's a mostly sunny day with a temperature of at least 60 degrees Fahrenheit. One advantage butterfly watching has over birding is that you can sleep in, since butterfly activity is usually best in the later morning, from about nine until noon. If, however, you also want to see some birds, you can get an early start and still have time to watch butterflies when the birding activity slows down.

Where to Find Them

Since butterflies usually need sugar energy to search for mates, you can find them anywhere that has an abundance of flowers for nectar and some open area where the sun can shine. Local flowers that especially attract butterflies include buckwheat (*Eriogonum*), wallflowers (*Erysimum*) and other mustards, thistles, asters and other sunflowers, yerba santa (*Eriodictyon*), mule fat (*Baccharis salicifolia*), dogbane (*Apocynum*), wild lilac (*Ceanothus*), mints (especially *Monardella*), milkweed (*Asclepias*), and nonnative lantana and zinnias. Many butterflies come to puddles to get needed minerals from mud or wet sand, so a stream running through an area, especially across an open trail or a dirt road, is always a plus.

Knowing the mating habits of butterflies can be helpful. A number of butterflies, including some swallowtails and the Desert Orangetip, go to local high points or ridges to search out mates, a behavior called hilltopping. Thus a climb to the top of some local hills is not only good exercise but can also be quite rewarding in terms of spotting butterflies.

Some butterflies never stray far from their food plants. The weak-flying Square-spotted and Dotted Blues nectar, search for mates, and lay eggs in and around the flower heads of their buckwheat food plants.

When you are looking for a specific butterfly, knowing its habitat preference and its food plant(s) is important. As you read through the species accounts in this book, you will note that most of the butterflies stick to specific habitats. If you want to see a Western Pine Elfin, you would not look in a Santa Monica neighborhood, even if the street was planted with many pine trees; though the Western Pine Elfin's food plant is pine, the butterfly is only found in our local mountains above 4,500 feet. Neither would you search out a 'Nelson's' Juniper Hairstreak atop Mount Baldy even though the species is found in the mountains; the hairstreak's food plant, incense cedar, does not grow at the highest reaches of our local mountains.

Southern California has a myriad of places and habitat types in which to look for butterflies, from your own well-watered backyard to the far reaches of our low-rainfall deserts; from below-sea-level agricultural areas in the Imperial Valley of Imperial County to the top of our highest mountain, Mount San Gorgonio, which reaches to 11,500 feet in the San Bernardino Mountains.

In the Species Accounts section of this book, we use area icons to define the general regions in Southern California that each butterfly inhabits. These icons and the general areas they indicate are as follows:

 DESERT: Many people imagine a desert as a place with sand dunes stretching as far as the eye can see. Although our deserts do have an occasional patch of sand dunes, they are hardly mere barren sand. Southern California has two different and unique deserts: the Mojave and the Colorado. The Mojave Desert, which encompasses eastern Kern County, northern Los Angeles County, and most of San Bernardino County, is called "high desert"—it is mostly over 2,000 feet in elevation. Bob's Gap, on the edge of Antelope Valley on the north side of the San Gabriel Mountains in Los Angeles County, is an excellent place to find many of the Mojave Desert butterflies, as is Mojave Narrows Regional Park in Victorville. Joshua Tree National Park is a little further afield; it is particularly interesting in that the Mojave and Colorado Deserts meet in the middle of the park. Thus you can find Mojave Desert species at Indian Cove in the northwest section of the park and Colorado Desert species around Cottonwood Spring in the southeast.

At the right time of year, Anza-Borrego Desert State Park in eastern San Diego County can be an excellent place to find Colorado Desert butterflies; Borrego Palm Canyon, Sentenac Canyon, Yaqui Well, and Plum Canyon are particularly good areas.

Mojave Desert

Colorado Desert

MOUNTAINS: Southern California has two major mountain range groupings. The east-west trending Transverse Ranges comprise, from west to east, the Santa Ynez, San Gabriel, and San Bernardino Mountains. The Santa Monica Mountains are a disjointed part of the Transverse Ranges, but because they barely reach above 3,000 feet, they don't have our typical mountain plant communities and butterflies. The Transverse Ranges, along with the Tehachapi Mountains, take most of the moisture out of the air from the Pacific Ocean in the form of rain and snow, making a rain shadow in the Mojave Desert.

The north-south trending Peninsular Ranges include, from north to south, the San Jacinto, Santa Rosa, Cuyamaca, and Laguna Mountains. The more westerly Santa Ana Mountains of Orange County are also considered part of the Peninsular Ranges. However, with not many peaks reaching over 5,000 feet, these mountains have a few plant communities of the lower mountain zones and no truly montane butterfly species. The Peninsular Ranges provide the rain shadow that creates the Colorado Desert.

Besides these ranges, there are a number of mountains far out in the Mojave Desert. This book does not thoroughly cover those mountains because of their distance from our population centers. Their unique location does make them home to a number of butterfly species and subspecies found nowhere else in Southern California.

The Tehachapi and Piute Mountains in Kern County link the Transverse Ranges with the southern Sierra Nevada. Although a number of subspecies reach their southern limits in these mountains, very few species there can't also be found in the Mount Piños area.

Our Southern California mountain plant communities are by no means uniform even at similar altitudes; they vary greatly with steepness, exposure (the direction they face), and the composition of the underlying soils. The lowest of our true mountain habitats starts at about 2,500 feet and is characterized by a scrubby chaparral (cold chaparral) or open pine forest where Coulter pine predominates. At about 4,500 feet, we enter an area formerly known as the transition zone, which may better be called the yellow pine belt, where Jeffrey and ponderosa pine predominate. At roughly 7,000 to 8,000 feet, a transition occurs to upper montane (formerly called the Canadian zone), where Jeffrey pine and white fir reign supreme. At about 9,500 feet, we reach an area once known as the Hudsonian zone, now better termed subalpine, where lodgepole pine becomes the

San Bernardino Mountains

dominant tree. Each of these zones has a somewhat unique assemblage of butterfly species associated with it. Finally, the treeless alpine zone occurs at the very top of Mount Baldy and Mount San Gorgonio. Since we have too little area in this zone to support a viable population, Southern California has no alpine butterflies.

The Angeles Crest Highway (State Highway 2), which starts in La Cañada Flintridge and goes through the San Gabriel Mountains, reaches almost 8,000 feet at its highest point. This is a great road to take if you want to sample our mountain butterflies; the mix of species changes as you climb in elevation. The many southward-facing canyons of the San Gabriel Mountains, such as Eaton, Santa Anita, Monrovia, San Gabriel, and Big Dalton, can be productive for butterflies. The Mount Piños area in the northeast corner of the Los Padres National Forest has a number of species hard to find elsewhere in Southern California.

Mountain meadows are always fine places to look for butterflies. The San Bernardino Mountains have a number of such meadows; Bluff Lake Meadow, a few miles south of Big Bear Lake, is one of the better ones. In San Diego County, the Laguna Mountains and Palomar Mountain State Park have numerous meadows that can yield many butterflies.

Coastal sage scrub

Chaparral

Oak woodland

COASTAL PLAIN: This area encompasses the Los Angeles Basin and all of cismontane (literally: this side of the mountains) Southern California up to 2,500 feet of elevation. The Santa Monica Mountains are mostly below 2,500 feet and thus are considered part of the coastal plain area.

Within this area, a number of different habitat types exist. One of the most prevalent is the coastal sage scrub, with indicator plants such as California sagebrush (*Artemisia californica*), California buckwheat (*Eriogonum fasciculatum*), several true sages (*Salvia*), a number of prickly pear cactuses (*Opuntia*), and shrubs such as lemonadeberry (*Rhus integrifolia*) and laurel sumac (*Malosma laurina*). A little higher in elevation, we find chaparral (warm chaparral) dominated by chamise (*Adenostoma fasciculatum*), with several species of wild lilacs (*Ceanothus*). Aside from these major habitats, we have a fair amount of oak woodland throughout our coastal plain. Unfortunately, Southern California's coastal salt marsh habitat has almost entirely disappeared due to development along our coasts.

The Santa Monica Mountains have a number of excellent spots to search for butterflies. These include La Jolla Canyon and Sycamore Canyon in Point Mugu State Park at the western end of the mountains; and Charmlee County Park and Malibu Creek State Park in Los Angeles County. Outside of the Santa Monica Mountains, O'Neill Regional Park in southern Orange County, Santa Rosa Plateau Preserve in Riverside County south of Lake Elsinore, and Mission Trails Regional Park in San Diego are all large areas of preserved natural habitats with wonderful opportunities for butterfly watching.

 RIPARIAN: The term for habitat areas along streams or rivers is *riparian*. Our deserts, mountains, and coastal plains all have riparian areas, each with a slightly different mix of dominant trees, but all mainly deciduous. Most riparian habitats have one or more species of willow (*Salix*). On our coastal plain, western sycamore (*Platanus racemosa*) grows along streams; in the desert, Fremont cottonwood (*Populus fremontii*) is more likely; and white alder (*Alnus rhombifolia*) predominates along our mountain streams.

A number of butterfly species occur close to streamsides because their food plants grow there. The riparian corridors also tend to attract and concentrate butterflies from nearby habitats. There are

Riparian woodland

two reasons for this: the availability of water allows plants to flower later in the season, offering nectar sources when those elsewhere have dried up; and the mud and wet sand at the stream edges bring in many butterflies for puddle parties, especially in the afternoon on hot summer days. Because we have such dry summers in Southern California, searching out riparian habitats wherever you look for butterflies will usually add to the total number of species you can see on a given day.

 GARDEN AND SUBURBAN: Southern California has a lot of well-watered gardens and lawns. As with riparian habitats, flowers and other plants continue to thrive here, drawing butterflies even after the summer heat has dried out our native habitats and vegetation. Gardens provide flowers for nectar and, in some cases, caterpillar food plants that stay edible throughout the summer. A number of our common skippers, such as the Fiery and Umber Skippers, use the grasses in our lawns as food plants. Caterpillars of butterflies such as the Western Tiger Swallowtail and the Mourning Cloak feed on the deciduous, broadleafed trees we plant for shade. If not for exotic garden plants such as passionvine (*Passiflora*)—the food plant of the Gulf Fritillary—and cassia (*Senna*), which feeds the Cloudless Sulphur, these butterflies would not exist in the Los Angeles Basin.

Home garden

Southern California has any number of urban gardens and parks that can be good to excellent places to find some of our more common butterflies that thrive in nonnative habitats. A few of the better spots are Descanso Gardens in La Cañada Flintridge, South Coast Botanic Garden on the Palos Verdes Peninsula, Huntington Central Park in Huntington Beach, and Balboa Park (especially the San Diego Zoo grounds) in San Diego.

When: Through the Seasons

Knowing when to look for butterflies is just as important as knowing where to look for them. A few butterflies can be found every month of the year in Southern California, including the Western Tiger Swallowtail, the Cabbage White, the Marine Blue, the Painted Lady, and the Fiery Skipper. However, most butterflies have a more limited flight time. Although a bird that is normally a summer resident, such as a Bullock's Oriole, might winter occasionally in our mild climate, you would never see a Boisduval's Blue outside of its late spring to midsummer flight period. Knowing when a particular species flies is key to finding it. Keep in mind that butterflies are dependent on the weather, especially rainfall. Below-average temperatures can delay flight times by several weeks, and higher-than-average temperatures can mean early flight times. In years of extremely low rainfall, the flights might not take place at all, or the number of individuals may be severely limited.

As the year progresses, different areas and times are better for butterflying; to see the maximum number of species in a year, plan your butterfly-watching trips with the following clues in mind. The following is a brief journey through the seasons.

LATE FEBRUARY TO MARCH The Colorado Desert, our low desert, comes alive with wildflowers as well as butterflies. The beautiful Sonoran Blue is an early flyer in the desert canyons, while the Bramble Hairstreak, the Sara and Desert Orangetips, the 'Loki' Juniper Hairstreak, and the California Patch start to appear and nectar on large flowering desert shrubs such as desert lavender and desert apricot. In a good flight year, the desert may be alive with thousands of migrating Painted Ladies moving north. One of the best places at this time of year is Anza-Borrego Desert State Park.

APRIL The Mojave Desert, our high desert, comes into bloom. Various white butterflies sometimes seem to dominate the landscape. If you look closely, you will see that these butterflies are not all the same; they can be Becker's, Cabbage, Spring, or Checkered Whites, as well as Pearly or Gray Marbles. Sagebrush Checkerspots appear on the floors of some canyon washes, while brightly colored Mormon Metalmarks search out buckwheats on which to nectar and lay eggs. At Bob's Gap, at the edge of the Mojave Desert on the north side of the San Gabriel Mountains in Los Angeles County, a number of desert habitats come together, hosting a good mix of butterflies. Joshua Tree National Park, with both the Colorado and Mojave Deserts within its boundaries, is a good place to look throughout the early spring.

MAY Some of the early butterflies, such as the Sara Orangetip, the Brown Elfin, the Silvery Blue, and the Funereal Duskywing, come out in our coastal lowlands starting in March and April, but May is the month when many local hairstreaks begin to fly. California buckwheat, a favorite for nectaring hairstreaks and many other butterflies, begins to bloom. Acmon and Square-spotted Blues, Gabb's and Variable Checkerspots, and West Coast and Painted Ladies are common or even abundant depending on the year. This is the best time of year for butterflying in our coastal canyons, from Santa Barbara south through the Santa Monica Mountains to San Diego.

JUNE The butterfly action starts to head upslope: our foothills and lower mountain canyon reaches become the ideal spots to find butterflies early in the month. The various southward-facing canyons of the San Gabriel Mountains are at their best at this time of year. The second brood of the Sara Orangetip is on the wing. Bright yellow 'Harford's' Queen Alexandra's Sulphurs and California Dogfaces make the days seem even sunnier. California and Mountain Mahogany Hairstreaks become common and the Tailed Copper can be locally abundant. The showy Lorquin's Admiral and California Sister dominate the trees above eye level. Boisduval's and Lupine Blues join other species to make field identification a bit more challenging. California buckwheat is still a major nectar source, along with yerba santa. As the day warms up, many species hang out at the edge of streams, imbibing minerals along with a little moisture.

JULY By this time the mountains are the place to see local butterflies as well as to escape the heat of the lowlands. Sometimes, the numerous Golden Hairstreaks seem to take over a canyon live oak, their food plant. This is the best time to find the beautifully marked Western Pine Elfin, and Greenish Blues reach peak numbers in the higher wet meadows. In the more open woodlands, you may see Great Basin Wood-Nymphs moving in and out of the shadows of trees and bushes with their characteristic weak, floppy flight.

AUGUST A lull in butterfly activity often occurs at this time of year. However, a number of local skippers become active, seeming to thrive on the heat. Because well-watered gardens provide many nectar flowers at this time of year, there may be more butterflies in our suburban habitats than in drier native habitats.

SEPTEMBER TO OCTOBER In years of good summer rains—usually thunderstorms—some desert areas bloom a second time, and a fall brood of butterflies takes advantage of the renewed nectar sources and food plants. Because these thunderstorms can occur quite locally, distribution of butterflies is often patchy. Along the coast, Monarchs start to congregate, nectaring on mule fat (*Baccharis salicifolia*) to store up enough energy to get through the winter. Queens turn up pretty regularly along the coast in the fall.

NOVEMBER TO FEBRUARY The only butterflies to appear in the winter months are those few species that fly throughout the year. This is a good time to visit the overwintering Monarch roosts in Southern California, the largest of which is just north of Santa Barbara.

Identification

Butterfly watching is going through a transition—the same one birding went through early in the last century. Before Roger Tory Peterson's *A Field Guide to Birds* came out, bird experts felt it wasn't possible to reliably identify birds by sight. Not too many years ago, Peterson himself was saying you couldn't tell our *Empidonax* (a genus of small look-alike flycatchers) species apart unless they sang. Much the same held true with butterflies only ten years ago. Many butterfly enthusiasts felt they needed a dead butterfly on a pin in order to identify some species with certainty. For other species, even that was not enough: they needed to examine the butterfly's genitalia. The Duskywings, a group of skippers, have the reputation of being notoriously difficult to identify, but butterflyers have managed to ferret out field marks we can reliably use to distinguish our six local species without having to dissect their genitalia.

Field identification problems still exist. The White Checkered-Skipper seems virtually indistinguishable from the Common Checkered-Skipper without genital examination. And, we still need to collect specimens to answer some questions, such as the exact nature of the Square-spotted/Dotted Blue taxonomy. It is important that we recognize unique species and subspecies that may need habitat protection.

This book will help you identify most of Southern California's common butterflies. However, not every local butterfly is pictured here. If you have a more serious interest and want to be able to identify every butterfly you find, especially the less common ones, you should add the two books listed at the end of this section to your library.

FAMILIES: Many beginning butterflyers, when they see a new butterfly, will flip through the pages of this book until they find a picture that matches it. This method works. To save some time and effort, however, you might first try to determine the butterfly's family. The task might seem easier knowing that Southern California has only six families: the swallowtails, the whites and sulphurs, the gossamer-wing butterflies, the metalmarks, the brushfooted butterflies, and the skippers. The Species Accounts section of this book includes a write-up on each family; here you can find information about approximate size, field marks, behaviors, and other distinguishing characteristics the family members share. Once you've practiced identifying butterflies by family, you can begin learning some of the subfamilies, such as the coppers, hairstreaks, and blues in the gossamer-wing family; the family write-ups also include information on subfamilies.

Of course, some butterflies will fool you. On seeing your first Mormon Metalmark, you might well identify it as a checkerspot in the brushfooted family. Don't be discouraged. Every butterfly expert today once went through the same learning experience.

COLOR AND PATTERN: The best way to identify a butterfly is to note its color and pattern and, using some knowledge of its family or subfamily, search through the pictures in the applicable section of the book. By confirming habitat and flight time (discussed below) you can usually make a reliable identification. However, for various reasons, your butterfly might not look exactly like the photograph in this or any other book. You may be seeing a worn butterfly that is not clearly marked. Depending on the species, males and females may be slightly to completely different. We have tried to picture both males and females when a strong sexual dimorphism— difference between male and female—exists. In some species, early and late broods vary in appearance. The Sara Orangetip is much brighter and more heavily marked in the first spring brood than in the later summer broods. The Common Ringlet also shows seasonal variation. Compare the photographs of the lightly marked summer individual and the darker early spring brood on page 211.

Butterfly subspecies with variations can develop. Butterflies are generally not strong flyers; most can't go great distances, so populations tend to become isolated when their required habitat is not continuous. This is especially true in the West, where high mountain ranges, wide deserts, or other geographical factors act as barriers. Once isolated, a population can evolve differently. Not many species in Southern California have two or more different-looking local subspecies. One exception is the aptly named Variable Checkerspot, which has several different subspecies in our area. One subspecies looks more like our local Edith's Checkerspot than the common subspecies of Variable Checkerspot.

Finally, occasional individuals have unusual variations of color or pattern, making identification quite a challenge. See page 183 for an example of such variation in a butterfly that is still clearly a Variable Checkerspot.

SIZE: In the Species Accounts section, you will find a normal size range for each butterfly listed under the Identification heading. The given size is the measurement from forewing tip to forewing tip. Because it is hard to visualize what a 1¾-inch butterfly (for instance) would look like, we suggest you familiarize yourself with the sizes of some of our more common butterflies. Then, when you see a butterfly in the field, you can make a mental comparison with a known butterfly. Some of the common butterflies you might use and their average sizes are: Marine Blue: ¾ inch; Fiery Skipper:

1 inch; Cabbage White: 1½ inches; Painted Lady: 2 inches; California Sister: 3 inches; and Monarch: 3¾ inches.

Note that females are larger than males, so that a female of our smallest species, the Western Pygmy-Blue, can sometimes be larger than a male Marine Blue. Rarely, you may come across a runt, which looks like a normal butterfly but much smaller. Authorities believe that in these cases, the caterpillar was not able to find enough of its food plant.

DISTRIBUTION: Although identifying birds depends to some degree on knowing where certain species are likely to be, distribution information is more important and more specific in regard to butterflies. NABA's *Checklist & English Names of North American Butterflies* lists over 700 species in North America north of Mexico. This number is somewhat comparable to the number of bird species in North America. However, whereas California boasts a list of more than 600 species of birds, it is home to just over 250 species of butterflies. In Southern California, the number of butterfly species drops to about 160. Contrast this with the almost 500 bird species recorded in Los Angeles County alone.

If North America has as many butterfly as bird species, why would we have so many fewer butterfly species locally? Part of the discrepancy is explained by the fact that butterflies are generally less mobile than birds. Many birds move in and out of our locale; we share our bird species with a wider area. With some exceptions (such as the Monarch or the Painted Lady), butterflies are sedentary, not venturing far from where they hatched as caterpillars. Many are tied to a specific food plant. The food plant, as discussed under Life Cycles above, is the plant the caterpillar (or larval stage) eats. Many butterflies nectar on a wide variety of flowers but are very particular about where they lay their eggs. The El Segundo Blue (an endangered subspecies of the Square-spotted Blue) both nectars and feeds on sea cliff buckwheat, so its distribution is limited to the few coastal sand dunes where the plant grows thickly.

The habitat requirements for each species tell you pretty specifically where to find those butterflies. While you might find a Pine or Magnolia Warbler at a remote desert oasis many miles from the nearest pine or magnolia tree, you would never expect to see a Pine White or a Mountain Mahogany Hairstreak more than a few hundred yards from the nearest pine or mountain mahogany, respectively. Since they are so similar, Square-spotted Blues and

Dotted Blues are difficult to separate, but because they are never far from their food plant, identifying the particular kind of buckwheat the butterfly is on helps significantly in identifying the butterfly. The Species Accounts section of this book includes photographs of many typical food plants. If you know the plant a butterfly is laying an egg on, you can use the food plant index to find which butterflies use this particular plant.

Wherever you are, the ecosystem type and the plants found there limit the number of butterfly species you might have to sort through to make an identification. This works the other way as well: when you are looking for a particular butterfly, it often helps if you start your search where the food plant grows.

To help you identify each butterfly, the Species Accounts section includes icons showing the general ecosystems a butterfly species inhabits, along with more specific habitat information and the species' food plant(s). This information can help clinch an identification when two similar-looking species are involved.

TEMPORAL CLUES: In addition to geographical and ecological clues, time of year is another key to determining a butterfly's identity. Many butterfly species fly only for a short time each year. The El Segundo Blue flies only from late June to early July, when the flower heads of the sea cliff buckwheat—the only food its caterpillars eat—are just beginning to appear. You can usually eliminate many butterfly species similar to the one you are trying to identify simply by knowing their flight times. Two fairly common grass skippers, the Rural Skipper and the Woodland Skipper, closely resemble each other, but their flight times overlap very little in our area: the Rural Skipper is primarily a spring butterfly, while the Woodland Skipper appears in the summer.

Flight times help experts, too, when they determine taxonomy: lepidopterists may formally reclassify some of the subspecies of the confusing Square-spotted and Dotted Blues as full species in the future, since the subspecies fly at different times—when their particular food plant is available.

The Species Accounts section of this book lists flight times as another aid to identification. When you go looking for butterflies, prepare yourself by finding out which butterflies might be flying at that time of year at your field destination.

OTHER BOOKS: We are extremely fortunate to have one of the very best local books on butterfly distribution: *The Butterflies of*

Southern California by Thomas and John Emmel. Since it sets out to cover only distribution, the book contains almost no identification information per se. It does, however, have ten color plates with photographs of specimens of each species and subspecies found in Southern California. Unfortunately, with so many butterflies on only ten plates, the individual images are about half of life size—a definite drawback for the smaller species. Still, it shows our local subspecies and has excellent information about where and when to find them, making it a valuable resource.

A few caveats about *The Butterflies of Southern California*: the common names in the book can be quite confusing, since many of them are specific to particular Southern California subspecies. The scientific names may be more helpful, but a number of these have changed since the book's publication in 1973. Some of the distribution information is also outdated. The Field Crescent is the most obvious example: it was scarce in our local mountains in 1973; it now appears to be totally extirpated in Southern California.

Southern California has been blessed with a number of more recent books that can help you identify local butterflies. The best book, however, is probably the more general *Butterflies through Binoculars: The West* by Jeffrey Glassberg, published in 2001. With this book alone, anyone can identify just about any Southern California butterfly, including those difficult skippers. Glassberg includes range maps opposite the photographs of each species. The only problem for the novice is that the book pictures over 450 species, making it hard to find the butterfly under observation before it flies away.

Organizations and Counts

A good way to learn more about Southern California butterflies is to meet other people interested in them who are willing to share their knowledge with you.

Members of the Lorquin Entomological Society have a broad interest in insects and spiders, and many are quite knowledgeable about our local butterflies. The group usually meets at the Natural History Museum of Los Angeles County on the fourth Friday in September, October, and January through April, and the first Friday in June and December.

The North American Butterfly Association (NABA) has local chapters in Southern California. You can find out where and when they meet through links on the NABA Web site, www.naba.org. Besides

butterflies. Joining and supporting any of these organizations is an excellent way to help ensure that future generations will enjoy an abundance of butterflies and butterfly species.

Endangered and Rare Species

The federal government currently lists four Southern California butterflies as endangered species. They are protected under the Endangered Species Act. The four are not actually full species, but subspecies found in extremely restricted ranges in Southern California. Each has very specific food plant requirements. They are: the Palos Verdes Blue (a subspecies of the Silvery Blue), the El Segundo Blue (a subspecies of the Square-spotted Blue), the Quino Checkerspot (a subspecies of the Edith's Checkerspot) and the Laguna Mountain Skipper (a subspecies of the Two-banded Checkered-Skipper).

The Palos Verdes Blue (see page 140) has an interesting story. Its food plant, California locoweed (*Astragalus trichopodus* var. *lonchus*), once thrived in the butterfly's habitat on the Palos Verdes Peninsula, but development has eliminated much of the native habitat. The Palos Verdes Blue was listed as endangered in 1980. In 1983, the city of Rancho Palos Verdes bulldozed the last known colony to make way for several baseball fields. A few years passed during which no sightings occurred, and authorities thought the butterfly was extinct.

Then, in 1994, while doing a biological survey at the U.S. Navy Fuel Storage Depot in San Pedro, three biologists stumbled upon a small colony. The Navy stopped work on a pipeline in the immediate area and allowed a restoration project to begin. In this limited-access area, workers have removed nonnative plants and planted locoweed and other native coastal sage scrub plants in an attempt to restore the native habitat. The project has helped the Palos Verdes Blue make a comeback. In the same area, the only remaining Los Angeles County population of the California Gnatcatcher, an endangered bird species also dependent on coastal sage scrub habitat, barely hangs on.

The El Segundo Blue (see page 134) also has a limited habitat. Its food plant, sea cliff buckwheat (*Eriogonum parvifolium*), grows profusely only in the remnant El Segundo sand dunes, which historically stretched from Marina del Rey to the Palos Verdes Peninsula. The largest of the El Segundo Blue's three separated colonies is on Los Angeles International Airport (LAX) property, between the airport runways and the beach. The area has restricted access and is off-limits to the public. LAX has funded native plant restoration for the butterflies, and the colony still thrives while the roaring jets take off just above it. However, airport expansion plans could jeopardize the colony, despite the protection of the Endangered Species Act.

Interestingly, when the airport originally bought the site, it was already mostly developed, with very little native habitat remaining—just enough sea cliff buckwheat to allow the butterfly colony to survive. LAX demolished the existing housing to avoid noise-related and safety liability issues. Conservationists thwarted later plans to build a golf course. Ironically, if not for LAX, development would have completely destroyed the dunes.

The other two El Segundo Blue colonies, both on private property, are much smaller than the LAX colony, with fewer than 100 butterflies each. Again, development has been the major factor in habitat loss.

The Quino Checkerspot (see page 184), yet another casualty of development, needs open areas of coastal sage scrub where its California plantain (*Plantago erecta*) food plant grows. The butterfly has been extirpated from Los Angeles and Orange Counties; only small colonies survive in as-yet undeveloped areas in western Riverside and San Diego Counties.

Our fourth endangered butterfly, the Laguna Mountain Skipper (mentioned on page 230), is the only one not directly threatened by development. Its habitat in the mountain meadows of San Diego County is mostly on protected state park and national forestland. However, its food plant, *Horkelia bolanderi,* grows best in open, disturbed areas. In the past, fires regularly cleared and rejuvenated the butterfly's habitat; Native Americans set some of these fires to provide open, grassy areas for the browsing deer they hunted. Fire suppression over the last century has decreased the open habitat the butterfly's food plant needs in order to grow.

Besides these four endangered subspecies, five full species are rarely found outside of Southern California: the Veined Blue, the California Giant-Skipper, the Hermes Copper, the San Emigdio Blue, and the Avalon Scrub-Hairstreak. The Veined Blue (see page 152), though limited in range, is probably in little danger since much of its habitat high in our local mountains (and in the southern Sierra Nevada) is protected as national forestland. The California Giant-Skipper (see page 250), has an even more restricted range along the western edge of the Colorado Desert in Riverside and San Diego counties and northern Baja California, Mexico. It is also probably safe since much of its habitat is protected in Anza-Borrego Desert State Park. The Hermes Copper (see page 92), on the other hand, has a limited range in coastal San Diego County and adjacent Mexico where development is extensive. This butterfly will probably need protection under the Endangered Species Act.

The San Emigdio Blue (see page 144) uses fourwing saltbush (*Atriplex canescens*) as its food plant, a common plant of our drier habitats; but the butterfly only occurs rarely in small colonies that extend north to the southern end of the Owens Valley. In the majority of its extensive potential habitat, development doesn't seem likely; however, a colony in the Canyon Country area of Los Angeles County was recently destroyed for housing.

The Avalon Scrub-Hairstreak (mentioned on page 118) has the most restricted range of these five species, only occurring on Santa Catalina Island. The Santa Catalina Island Conservancy plans to ensure the preservation of plenty of native habitat for this species. However, another threat to the butterfly's existence is the closely related Gray Hairstreak, which has recently colonized Santa Catalina Island and is reportedly hybridizing with the Avalon Scrub-Hairstreak. Eventually, if the isolating mechanisms between the two species are not strong enough, a butterfly that is predominantly a Gray Hairstreak might replace the Avalon Scrub-Hairstreak.

A NOTE FROM THE PHOTOGRAPHER

I discovered the intriguing world of butterflies after many years of enjoying a modicum of success photographing birds. However, my endeavors to photograph these marvelous insects in the wild presented quite a challenge. After much trial and error, I have settled on the following techniques. Keep in mind that there is no right or wrong way to accomplish your own goals in photography. Other photographers have taken many excellent pictures of butterflies using methods that, for various reasons, I do not employ.

Use the highest quality equipment you can afford. Unfortunately, good equipment is not cheap. But if you are as severe a critic of the results as I am, the financial investment is worthwhile.

I find butterfly photography a little easier than bird photography because the equipment required is simpler and more portable. Presently, for butterflies I use a Nikon F-100 camera body with a Nikon 200mm micro 1:1 ratio lens. I always use a flash because ambient or natural lighting usually is not sufficient to stop motion or obtain enough depth of field. My flash is an SB-28 Nikon mounted on the camera and fitted with an SD-8 battery pack for faster recycling. I never use a tripod as it just gets in the way. I shoot slide film; Fujichrome Sensia ISO 100 is my current favorite. This setup provides a fair amount of working distance, allowing me to move about for better camera angles. The shutter speed is set at 1/200 or 1/250 depending on the brightness of the background. The lens opening is generally set around f/22. I try to avoid black backgrounds. The light of the flash (about 1/1000 second) provides the main illumination of the subject, while the camera controls the total amount of light actually reaching the film using TTL (through the lens) metering.

Of course there are the usual frustrations, among which are such problems as frightening away the subject by some clumsy move, wanting the dorsal view while the butterfly keeps its wings closed, or wanting the ventral view when the wings are held open. Usually I only photograph live butterflies in the wild, and my subjects are not touched or restrained in anyway. However, there is one exception in this book. The picture of the dorsal view of the male California Dogface is of a museum specimen. It is used for illustrative purposes because I have not yet been able take such a photograph in the wild.

Entering this new world has been a source of tremendous satisfaction to me. I hope you enjoy viewing the results of my efforts in this book while you read and learn about these fascinating creatures.

SPECIES ACCOUNTS

This section contains descriptions and photographs of eighty-nine species of Southern California butterflies. Each species listing uses the format below.

Butterfly Name

Each species is designated by its common English name followed by its scientific name in italics. Both names accord with the second edition of the *Checklist & English Names of North American Butterflies*, published in 2001 by the North American Butterfly Association (NABA). Superfamily, family, and subfamily designations, as well as the order in which the species are presented, also follow this checklist.

Area Icons

One or more area icons indicate the types of habitat where you might find the butterfly in Southern California:

Throughout

The sun icon is used for butterflies that can be found all over Southern California in many different habitats, thus anywhere under the sun. These species include such common butterflies as the Cabbage White, Orange Sulphur, Marine Blue, Painted Lady, and Fiery Skipper. Although these butterflies can be found throughout Southern California, some are more likely to be seen in particular areas and thus may have additional icons.

Desert

Southern California has two distinct deserts: the high Mojave Desert north of the Transverse Ranges and the low Colorado Desert east of the Peninsular Ranges.

Mountains

This comprises most of the mountains in Southern California above 2,500 feet. (Because the highest point in the Santa Monica Mountains is just over 3,000 feet, butterflies found there are listed as coastal plains species.) The mountain habitats occur mostly in the east-west-trending Transverse Ranges (Santa Ynez, San Gabriel, and San Bernardino Mountains) and the north-south-trending Peninsular Ranges (San Jacinto, Santa Rosa, and Laguna Mountains, as well as the lower and more western Santa Ana Mountains). Also included are the higher mountains of the Mojave Desert such as the Clark, Providence, and New York Mountains.

Coastal Plain

The coastal plain includes all lowland areas from the immediate coast to the foothills and canyons of our local mountains up to roughly 2,500 feet. This area is sometimes referred to as cismontane ("this side of the mountains") and includes the areas south of the Transverse Ranges (the Santa Ynez, San Gabriel, and San Bernardino Mountains) and west of the Peninsular Ranges (the San Jacinto, Santa Rosa, and Laguna Mountains). The Santa Monica Mountains, which lie mainly below 2,500, are included here.

Riparian

Riparian habitats are those along streams or rivers, whether in the mountains, on coastal plains, or even in deserts. Thus the riparian icon usually appears alongside one or more other area icons. The specific plants that grow in riparian habitats or the availability of water are key attractants for many butterfly species.

Garden, Urban, or Suburban

This icon is used for butterflies that frequent human-made, nonnative habitats. Most of these butterflies inhabit natural areas, but food plants, nectar sources, and water draw them to our lawns, gardens, and even weedy lots. Some actually depend heavily on humans and would be here not at all or in reduced numbers without our help. For example, the Gulf Fritillary's food plants are exotic passionvines grown in many backyard gardens. The Fiery Skipper uses such nonnative flowers as lantana for a nectar source, and its caterpillar feeds on lawn grasses.

Habitat

The area icons give only a general idea of where you might find each species. The habitat description provides more specific information on the butterfly's requirements.

Flight Time

This is a range of months during which you may see the adult butterfly. You may not find the butterfly every year, especially during the early or late months of its flight time. A cold spring, for example, may delay the emergence of a species for a month or more; conversely, a dry spring and hot summer may see a flight end early. In our mild Southern California climate, a number of species can be found all year long, but even these tend to be scarce in winter.

Broods

Butterfly populations go through one or more complete life cycles during a year. The number of broods a species produces in a year can depend on climate: some types of butterflies may have only a single cycle a year in the far north, but two or more broods in warmer southern areas. The number shown—1, 2, or M (designating *multiple* for more than two broods)—is the normal number of broods each species produces in Southern California. A few desert species may have a fall brood only when summer rains are good. In dry years, some species may not emerge at all.

Overwintering

The icon indicates at which stage in a species' life cycle it spends the winter. The technical term for this period of relative inactivity is *diapause*. The following icons appear:

Egg

Caterpillar

Pupa (or chrysalis)

Adult

For a few species, we do not yet know at what stage they overwinter. These species will have no icon.

Food Plant

A species' food plants are the plants its caterpillars feed on. Adult females lay their eggs on or near this plant. The plant you see a butterfly on may be its food plant; even the proximity of likely food plants can sometimes help you identify the butterfly. Because common English names for plants can vary, we have sometimes added the scientific name for a plant's family, genus, or species in parentheses, for clarity. The genus and species are always in italics, while the family name is in regular type. When a plant has no generally accepted English name, the scientific name alone is given. All scientific names follow *The Jepson Manual: Higher Plants of California* (see Suggested Resources, page 263).

Nectar Plant

Nectar is a source of energy for the adult butterfly. Many butterflies have favorite flowers from which they nectar regularly. However, species do not adhere as rigidly to their choice of nectar plants as they do to the food plants for their caterpillars, and butterflies are more apt to use substitutes when their favored nectar plants are not available. Thus, unlike with food plants, nectar plants are not a reliable aid to identification. They are, however, good places to look for butterflies. A number of butterflies seldom nectar or don't seem to visit any particular flowers regularly. For these species no nectar plant is listed.

Introductory Paragraph

This section gives information on such things as abundance and status in Southern California, camouflage, migration, mate finding, life cycle stages, and other interesting facts about the butterfly.

Identification

The identification box contains a few pointers on how to distinguish the species from other similar butterflies. Note that while this book can help you identify many of the commonly encountered species, it is not a detailed guide to field marks or to distinguishing difficult species. For those people interested in detailed butterfly identification, the Suggested Resources section lists a number of books better suited for this purpose. Finally, the range of the species size in inches from forewing tip to forewing tip is found at the end of this section.

IDENTIFICATION FEATURES

Submargin

Margin

Postmedian

Median

Forewing

Trailing Corner

Postmedian

Median

Hindwing

View below

View above

Postmedian

Median

Forewing

Trailing Edge

Hindwing

Submargin

Margin

Apex or Wing Tip

Two-tailed Swallowtail

SWALLOWTAILS
Family Papilionidae

Swallowtails are the largest butterflies in Southern California. Their large size, bright colors, and slow, graceful flight make them the most commonly noticed of our local butterflies. Most butterflies in this family have tail-like projections from the tip of their hindwings; these give the family its name. The tails look somewhat like antennae, and many species have eyespots on the hindwings (see the photograph of the Black Swallowtail on page 57), making the hind end resemble a head. In addition, patterns on the wings help direct a viewer's eyes towards the tail end. This head-to-tail mimicry can trick a predator such as a bird into striking the back end of the butterfly, allowing the insect to escape with nothing more damaging than a piece taken out of its wing.

When nectaring, swallowtails tend to flutter continuously, making it hard to get a decent photo or a good look at pattern details. In a number of swallowtail species, males seek out a hill or mountaintop where they await unmated females. This behavior leads to a concentration of butterflies, making them easier to find even when the overall density in an area is somewhat low.

In their early stages, the caterpillars of many swallowtails resemble bird droppings, which makes them hard to spot. All swallowtail caterpillars have a foul-smelling gland called the osmeterium; the caterpillar can extend this gland from the back of its head to deter predators. In general, swallowtail caterpillars feed on broad-leafed deciduous trees and members of the carrot family.

Nine species of swallowtails are found in Southern California.

'Desert' Black Swallowtail

Papilio polyxenes coloro

Habitat: Open desert, especially along washes

Flight Time: February through October

Broods: M

Food Plant: Turpentine broom (*Thamnosma montana*); citrus on occasion.

Nectar: Thistle and other aster family members; also chuparosa (*Beloperone californica*)

After good winter rains, this butterfly can be quite common in the spring in our local deserts. Summer thunderstorms can also bring out a decent fall flight. Conversely, during drought conditions, the pupa can delay emergence for several years. The Black Swallowtail ranges all the way to the East Coast. Some authorities consider the subspecies of the Black Swallowtail that occurs from our local deserts to southern Nevada and western Arizona a separate species. Anza-Borrego Desert State Park in March and Joshua Tree National Park are two good places to observe this species.

IDENTIFICATION

The wide yellow median band on both wings and the desert habitat distinguish this species from all other local swallowtails. However, at the desert edges, the range of this swallowtail overlaps a little with that of the similar looking Anise Swallowtail (*Papilio zelicaon*). The yellow forewing marginal spots are rounder in the Black Swallowtail and more flattened in the Anise Swallowtail. The Black Swallowtail's appearance is somewhat variable; those in the eastern Mojave Desert tend to have a much reduced yellow median band, which could cause it to be confused with the rare 'Martin's' subspecies of the Indra Swallowtail (*Papilio indra martini*) also found there.

Size: 2 3/8 to 3 inches

'Desert' Black Swallowtail

Turpentine broom

Anise Swallowtail
Papilio zelicaon

Habitat: Varied, but generally open areas
Flight Time: All year
Broods: M
Food Plant: Sweet fennel (*Foeniculum vulgare*), citrus (can be a pest), and parsley or other carrot family (Apiaceae) members
Nectar: Thistle, lantana

This butterfly uses many native plants from the carrot family as food plants. However, because it now also uses the introduced sweet fennel (or wild anise) plant, the Anise Swallowtail is probably more common than ever. The caterpillars eat both the fennel's young leaves and flower buds. The Anise Swallowtail, like many of its family, is a hilltopper; look for it on local open hilltops. One such site where Anise Swallowtails regularly congregate is tiny Del Cerro Park on the Palos Verdes Peninsula.

IDENTIFICATION

The desert-dwelling Black Swallowtail (see previous species) resembles the Anise Swallowtail, but their different habitat requirements usually keep them separate. The Old World Swallowtail (previously called Baird's Swallowtail) also looks like this species, but it is slightly larger and is restricted to the San Bernardino Mountains. The uncommon Indra Swallowtail has several races in our area, some quite rare, but their yellow median band is much narrower.

Size: 2 ⅝ to 3 inches

Anise Swallowtail

Sweet fennel

Anise Swallowtail caterpillar

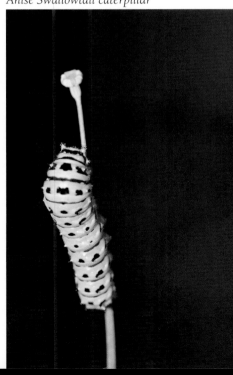

Giant Swallowtail
Papilio cresphontes

Habitat: Wherever citrus trees grow
Flight Time: March through October
Broods: M
Food Plant: Citrus

In the early 1970s, the Giant Swallowtail occurred in our area only along the Colorado River, where its caterpillars fed on the new shoots and leaves of citrus trees. During the 1990s, it spread west and north and became a rather common butterfly in Orange County. Its range has now expanded into Los Angeles County, and it will certainly show up in Ventura County before long. Because of its food plant choice, citrus growers there will not welcome it. The farmers call Giant Swallowtail caterpillars "Orange Dogs."

IDENTIFICATION

Its pattern of yellow bands and its large size make this butterfly unmistakable.

Size: 3⅜ to 5½ inches

Giant Swallowtail

Lemon tree

Western Tiger Swallowtail
Papilio rutulus

Habitat: Varied

Flight Time: All year

Broods: M

Food Plant: Most commonly sycamore; also poplar, cottonwood, willow, and alder

Nectar: Thistle, lantana, zinnia and other aster family members, yerba santa (*Eriodictyon*)

This species is one of the largest of our Southern California butterflies. Its bright yellow color never fails to delight as it glides through gardens and along suburban streets. Its food plants are broad-leafed deciduous trees such as sycamores, cottonwoods, willows, and alders, many of which grow naturally along streamsides or have been planted in suburban neighborhoods. The Western Tiger Swallowtail is a strong flyer, so you may see it almost anywhere. The male searches for mates by gliding up and down streambeds. These swallowtails congregate at mud puddles along the same watercourses. The Western Tiger Swallowtail is the most widely noticed of our local butterflies; people sometimes mistakenly assume it is a Monarch.

IDENTIFICATION

The Pale Swallowtail also has the "tiger stripes" (actually bands) that give the Western Tiger Swallowtail its name, but the Pale Swallowtail is more of a creamy white with thicker black bands and is less likely to be found in a garden. The very similar Two-tailed Swallowtail is far less common and is occasionally found on the north slopes of local mountains from Mount Piños to Wrightwood. It is slightly bigger and, true to its name, has two tails on each wing.

Size: 2¾ to 3⅞ inches

Western Tiger Swallowtail

Western Tiger Swallowtail

Pale Swallowtail
Papilio eurymedon

Habitat: Chaparral and foothill canyons
Flight Time: February through October
Broods: M
Food Plant: Wild lilacs (*Ceanothus*); holly-leafed cherry (*Prunus ilicifolia*); buckthorn, coffeeberry, redberry (all *Rhamnus*)
Nectar: Thistle, mint, wallflower, yerba santa (*Eriodictyon*)

This common butterfly is likely to be found in the wilder areas of our native habitat and not in the suburban settings normally frequented by the Western Tiger Swallowtail. The native habitat is more likely to have the food plants upon which the caterpillars of the Pale Swallowtail feed. The males of the Pale Swallowtail are hilltoppers and search out mates by patrolling on hilltops and the highest peaks in Southern California. Pale Swallowtails can be abundant in the late spring and early summer at such places as Mount Piños in Ventura County, Mount Baden-Powell in Los Angeles County, and Garnet Peak in the Laguna Mountains of San Diego County. These butterflies are regularly seen nectaring on flowers and coming to mud puddles.

IDENTIFICATION

This species can only be confused with the Western Tiger Swallowtail, which has a similar pattern. The Pale Swallowtail, as its name suggests, is a paler cream color (rather than bright yellow) with heavier black bands.

Size: 3 to 3¾ inches

Pale Swallowtail

Pale Swallowtail

Chaparral whitethorn

Spring White

A puddle party in Arizona mainly made up of Mexican Yellows, with a few other speci
such as Southern Dogface, Tailed Orange, Sleepy Orange, and a non-Pierid Bordered Pat

Orange Sulphur female ("alba" form)

Orange Sulphur male

California Dogface
Colias eurydice

Habitat: Foothills with chaparral or oak woodlands
Flight Time: February through October
Broods: 2
Food Plant: False indigo (*Amorpha californica*)
Nectar: Purple flowers especially, including yerba santa (*Eriodictyon*)

The California Dogface is California's official state butterfly. It gets its name from the pattern on the upper forewing, which resembles a poodle's face. The pale spot on the forewing below is a dark spot above and looks like an eye; the face's nose points to the outer edge of the wing. Unfortunately, these butterflies seldom land with their wings open, making it difficult to get a good photograph of the distinctive upper surface. The following photo of the male above is of a specimen from the collection of the Natural History Museum of Los Angeles County. It is the only photo of a nonliving butterfly in this book and is included because the California Dogface is the state butterfly and is quite beautiful and distinctive.

California Dogfaces come regularly to mud and are sometimes seen in large puddle parties. The southward-facing canyons of the San Gabriel Mountains, including Monrovia, San Gabriel, and Big Dalton Canyons, are all excellent places to find this butterfly in the late spring. Both this species and the Southern Dogface are found on the desert side of the San Bernardino Mountains, where they hybridize regularly.

IDENTIFICATION

The term *falcate* is used to describe the pointed fore-wings of the California Dogface. This feature differentiates the plain yellow or off-white females from the similar Cloudless Sulphur. At the desert edges of Southern California, both the male and female Southern Dogface have a pattern and wing shape similar to those of the male California Dogface. However the Southern Dogface has a lemon yellow background, while the California Dogface's is more of a golden yellow with a purple sheen on the forewings above.

Size: 1⅞ to 2½ inches

California Dogface male

California Dogface museum specimen

Cloudless Sulphur
Phoebis sennae

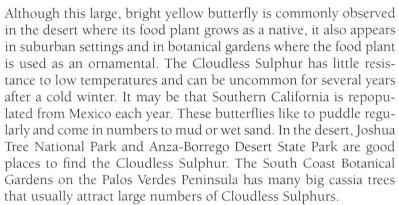

Habitat: Wherever cassia—its food plant—grows, especially deserts
Flight Time: February through December
Broods: M
Food Plant: Native and nonnative cassia (*Senna*)
Nectar: Thistle

Although this large, bright yellow butterfly is commonly observed in the desert where its food plant grows as a native, it also appears in suburban settings and in botanical gardens where the food plant is used as an ornamental. The Cloudless Sulphur has little resistance to low temperatures and can be uncommon for several years after a cold winter. It may be that Southern California is repopulated from Mexico each year. These butterflies like to puddle regularly and come in numbers to mud or wet sand. In the desert, Joshua Tree National Park and Anza-Borrego Desert State Park are good places to find the Cloudless Sulphur. The South Coast Botanical Gardens on the Palos Verdes Peninsula has many big cassia trees that usually attract large numbers of Cloudless Sulphurs.

The Cloudless Sulphur caterpillar forms a tent with the leaves of its food plant and holds it together using excreted silk threads.

IDENTIFICATION

In the desert, the large, unmarked, bright yellow Cloudless Sulphur shouldn't be confused with anything else. Females usually have some dark on the wing edges and aren't quite as bright a yellow; they can even be off-white. Below, both sexes generally have some small wavy lines and two silver spots on the hindwing, though these may be indistinct on the male.

In our mountains, the largely unmarked yellow female California Dogface can look like a Cloudless Sulphur, but the latter is rarely found there.

Size: 2 ¼ to 2 ¾ inches

Cloudless Sulphur male

Spiny senna

Sleepy Orange
Eurema nicippe

Habitat: Wherever cassia—the food plant—grows
Flight Time: All year
Broods: M
Food Plant: Native and nonnative cassia (*Senna*)

The distribution of the vividly colored Sleepy Orange is similar to that of the Cloudless Sulphur, which uses the same food plant, but the Sleepy Orange is usually less common in Southern California. Also like the Cloudless Sulphur, the Sleepy Orange may be repopulated from Mexico every year. The name probably comes from a marking on the forewing above that resembles a mostly closed eye. You can often find Sleepy Oranges puddling at springs in the desert. One of the best places to observe this behavior is at Cottonwood Spring in Joshua Tree National Park.

IDENTIFICATION

This medium-sized, glowing orange butterfly with black wing margins is hard to misidentify, even in flight. When it lands, you can see its golden yellow undersides, sometimes with heavy rust-colored markings. In the winter months, the undersides are darker and browner. The hindwing is marked with a diagonal bar near the center and a vertical bar on the front edge.

In flight the Sleepy Orange resembles a male Orange Sulphur, but the Sleepy Orange is a much deeper orange and flies weakly, low to the ground.

Size: 1⅜ to 1⅞ inches

Sleepy Orange

Sleepy Orange with rust-colored markings.

Dainty Sulphur
Nathalis iole

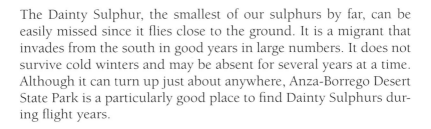

Habitat: Usually lowlands, but also open dryer areas in our mountains

Flight Time: March through November

Broods: M

Food Plant: Sneezeweed (*Helenium*), beggar's tick (*Bidens*), marigold and other sunflower family (Asteraceae) members

The Dainty Sulphur, the smallest of our sulphurs by far, can be easily missed since it flies close to the ground. It is a migrant that invades from the south in good years in large numbers. It does not survive cold winters and may be absent for several years at a time. Although it can turn up just about anywhere, Anza-Borrego Desert State Park is a particularly good place to find Dainty Sulphurs during flight years.

IDENTIFICATION

This small, low-flying, pale yellow butterfly with dark wing tips is unmistakable. When one lands on the ground or on a low flower, its small size and the dull markings on its hindwing below help it blend into its surroundings. If the forewing below is exposed, the yellowish center and submarginal spots are a giveaway.

Size: ¾ to 1¼ inches

Dainty Sulphur

Bigelow's sneezeweed

GOSSAMER-WING BUTTERFLIES
Family Lycaenidae

Most of the Lycaenidae are small butterflies; the Western Pygmy-Blue is one of the smallest in the world. Many gossamer-wings have intricate patterns and are among the most beautiful of our butterflies. This family consists of three subfamilies: the coppers (Lycaeninae) and blues (Polyommatinae), which are named primarily for their colors above, and the hairstreaks (Theclinae), named for their hairlike hindwing projections. However, Southern California has a blue with no blue in the wings, a copper that is bright blue above, and a number of tailless hairstreaks, as well as a copper and a blue with tails. Although these exceptions can cause confusion, practiced butterfly watchers can sort most of the gossamer-wings into the correct subfamily fairly easily.

The gossamer-wings usually land with their wings closed, so observers generally see only the undersides. Luckily, most species have diagnostic markings below that make identification fairly straightforward. Because of the small size of these butterflies, close-focusing binoculars are very helpful, especially in seeing the exquisite details on some of our hairstreaks.

The flight of these little butterflies is quick and erratic, and although they don't usually go far, they are sometimes hard to follow with the eye. Most of them are avid nectarers. Once they settle down on a flower, they will generally stay put, allowing a good look.

The pattern on many hairstreaks gives them some protection from predators such as birds. Hairstreaks tend to face slightly downward, and their tails resemble antennae. In addition, many have large spots in the corner of the hindwing that look like eyes, further adding to the illusion of the head being at the tail end. Quite often you can find hairstreaks with portions of their hindwings in the vicinity of the tail bitten off.

The caterpillars usually eat the flowers or buds of plants and sometimes even the fruit. A number of blue and hairstreak caterpillars

Golden Hairstreak

Golden Hairstreak on canyon live oak food plant

Great Purple Hairstreak
Atlides halesus

Habitat: A wide range of habitats where its food plant grows on various tree types

Flight Time: February through November

Broods: M

Food Plant: Mistletoe (*Phoradendron*) on cottonwoods and sycamores along streams, on mesquite and ironwood in the desert, and on juniper and pines elsewhere

Nectar: Buckwheat (*Eriogonum*), sunflower family members, and desert lavender (*Hyptis emoryi*)

This beautifully colored butterfly is the largest of our Southern California hairstreaks. Its name doesn't seem to make sense, since the butterfly is a bright iridescent blue above and definitely not purple. Usually, Great Purple Hairstreaks remain high in the trees where their mistletoe food plant is generally found. They frequently come down to nectar on various flowers, allowing observers to closely approach. They twitch their tails while nectaring, probably to fool predators by adding to the illusion that the back end is actually the head. Occasionally, you will find a Great Purple Hairstreak with a bird-beak-shaped portion missing from the hindwing, proving that this deception works well. The pupa is usually hidden in leaf litter at the base of a tree or in the bark.

IDENTIFICATION

At a distance, the Great Purple Hairstreak appears to be a dark, small- to medium-sized butterfly, unlike any other in Southern California. From closer-up, one notices the green and red spots on the hindwings below, the long black tails, and the orange abdomen that confirm the identification.

Size: 1¼ to 1½ inches

Great Purple Hairstreak

Desert mistletoe

Behr's Hairstreak
Satyrium behrii

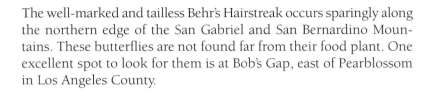

Habitat: Dry slopes on the desert edges in juniper—Joshua tree woodlands

Flight Time: June through July

Broods: 1

Food Plant: Antelope brush (*Purshia tridentata*)

Nectar: Buckwheat (*Eriogonum*)

The well-marked and tailless Behr's Hairstreak occurs sparingly along the northern edge of the San Gabriel and San Bernardino Mountains. These butterflies are not found far from their food plant. One excellent spot to look for them is at Bob's Gap, east of Pearblossom in Los Angeles County.

IDENTIFICATION

The Behr's Hairstreak is easy to identify: it is brown below with heavy black-and-white markings, and it has no tails. Above, the back half of the forewing and most of the hindwing are a dull orange, apparent in flight on this weakly flying butterfly.

Size: ⅞ to 1⅛ inches

Behr's Hairstreak

Mojave antelope brush

California Hairstreak
Satyrium californica

Habitat: Oak woodland and chaparral
Flight Time: May through August
Broods: 1
Food Plant: Wild lilac (*Ceanothus*) and oak (*Quercus*)
Nectar: Buckwheat (*Eriogonum*) and yerba santa (*Eriodictyon*)

This is a common butterfly in our higher local mountains and is found regularly nectaring at roadside flowers. The caterpillars eat only the leaves of the food plant and are usually attended by ants offering protection in exchange for the honeydew the caterpillars exude.

IDENTIFICATION

The California Hairstreak is mostly dull brown above with dusky orange patches at the trailing margin of the hindwing. It is similar to the Sylvan Hairstreak (*Satyrium sylvinus*), which is more lightly marked and paler below, with less orange on the margin. The Sylvan Hairstreak is restricted to riparian habitats where its willow food plant grows.

Size: 1 to 1¼ inches

California Hairstreak

Sylvan Hairstreak

Mountain Mahogany Hairstreak
Satyrium tetra

Habitat: Chaparral
Flight Time: May through July
Broods: 1
Food Plant: Mountain mahogany (*Cercocarpus betuloides*)
Nectar: California buckwheat (*Eriogonum fasciculatum*)
and yerba santa (*Eriodictyon*)

The Mountain Mahogany Hairstreak can be an extremely common butterfly in the chaparral where its food plant occurs. It comes readily to flowers—especially California buckwheat—for nectar. Many older books refer to this butterfly as the Gray Hairstreak (although it is really gray brown), leading to confusion with the truly gray butterfly that has that name today. The Gray Hairstreak (*Strymon melinus*) is known in those same books as the Common Hairstreak.

IDENTIFICATION

Gray brown above, the Mountain Mahogany Hairstreak resembles a couple of the other chaparral hairstreaks below: the Gold-hunter's (*Satyrium auretorum*) and the Hedgerow (*Satyrium saepium*). However, the Mountain Mahogany is much grayer below, with white frosting beyond the white postmedian line on the hindwing. In addition, its forewing is somewhat pointed, making it appear taller when perched on a flower.

Size: 1⅛ to 1¼ inches

Mountain Mahogany Hairstreak

Mountain mahogany

Hedgerow Hairstreak

Satyrium saepium

Habitat: Foothill and mountain chaparral
Flight Time: April through July
Broods: 1
Food Plant: Wild lilac (*Ceanothus*)
Nectar: California buckwheat (*Eriogonum fasciculatum*), yerba santa (*Eriodictyon*), and wild lilac

Our most common chaparral hairstreak, the Hedgerow can be quite abundant, with many individuals nectaring on a single California buckwheat plant in the proper habitat.

IDENTIFICATION

Below, the Hedgerow Hairstreak is plain brown with a postmedian band consisting of white and black bars and a blue gray spot in the trailing corner of the hindwing. This coloration contrasts with the similar but more dully marked Gold-hunter's Hairstreak (*Satyrium auretorum*). Above, the Hedgerow Hairstreak is a rusty orange that is obvious in the flying butterfly and immediately sets it apart from the Gold-hunter's.

Size: 1 to 1⅛ inches

Hedgerow Hairstreak

Gold-hunter's Hairstreak

Bramble Hairstreak
Callophrys dumetorum

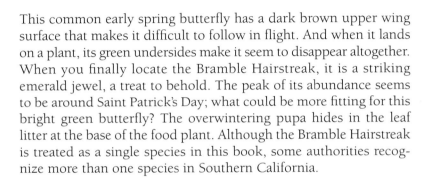

Habitat: Coastal sage scrub and chaparral to the desert edge

Flight Time: February through April

Broods: 1

Food Plant: Deerweed *(Lotus scoparius)*, wild lilac *(Ceanothus)*, and buckwheat *(Eriogonum)*

Nectar: California buckwheat *(Eriogonum fasciculatum)*

This common early spring butterfly has a dark brown upper wing surface that makes it difficult to follow in flight. And when it lands on a plant, its green undersides make it seem to disappear altogether. When you finally locate the Bramble Hairstreak, it is a striking emerald jewel, a treat to behold. The peak of its abundance seems to be around Saint Patrick's Day; what could be more fitting for this bright green butterfly? The overwintering pupa hides in the leaf litter at the base of the food plant. Although the Bramble Hairstreak is treated as a single species in this book, some authorities recognize more than one species in Southern California.

IDENTIFICATION

The 'Desert' Sheridan's Hairstreak *(Callophrys sheridanii comstocki)*, which lives far out in the Mojave Desert, is similar to the Bramble Hairstreak, but the 'Desert' Sheridan's hindwing below has a distinctive strong white postmedian band with an outward bulge.

Size: ⁷⁄₈ to 1¹⁄₈ inches

Bramble Hairstreak

Deerweed

Brown Elfin
Callophrys augustinus

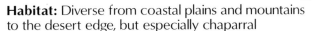

Habitat: Diverse from coastal plains and mountains to the desert edge, but especially chaparral

Flight Time: February through July

Broods: 1

Food Plant: Mainly dodder (*Cuscuta*), but also wild lilac (*Ceanothus*), soap plant (*Chlorogalum pomeridianum*), and Pacific madrone (*Arbutus menziesii*)

Nectar: California buckwheat *(Eriogonum fasciculatum)*

This somewhat uncommon spring butterfly has an unusually wide choice of habitats and food plants. The caterpillars feed on the buds and flowers of the food plants.

IDENTIFICATION

The little projection at the trailing corner of the hindwing is fairly distinctive on this small, mostly warm brown butterfly. Only the Moss' Elfin (*Callophrys mossii*) is similar, but it is slightly more clearly marked below and in Southern California is found only in a few mountain canyons where its food plant, stonecrop (*Sedum spathulifolium*), grows.

Size: ¾ to 1⅛ inches

Brown Elfin

Dodder

Western Pine Elfin

Callophrys eryphon

Habitat: Pine forest
Flight Time: May through July
Broods: 1
Food Plant: Pine (*Pinus*)
Nectar: Many and varied flowers

This uniquely marked butterfly is only found high up in our local mountains where its food plant grows abundantly. The caterpillar feeds on the young, tender pine needles.

IDENTIFICATION

The markings below, especially the darker zigzag sub-marginal line on the hindwing, make this butterfly unmistakable.

Size: ¾ to 1¼ inches

Western Pine Elfin

Yellow pine forest

Juniper Hairstreak
Callophrys gryneus

The Juniper Hairstreaks are a complex of closely related butterflies that feed on trees in the cypress family (juniper, cypress, and cedar). According to some authorities, they may in fact be different species. Southern California has four distinct subspecies, discussed in the next few pages. When viewed up close, these hairstreaks are among the most beautiful in our area.

'Nelson's' Juniper Hairstreak
Callophrys gryneus nelsoni

Habitat: Midlevel pine forest with incense cedar
Flight Time: May through July
Broods: 1
Food Plant: Incense cedar (*Calocedrus decurrens*)
Nectar: Buckwheat (*Eriogonum*) and whitethorn (*Ceanothus*)

This very territorial butterfly usually stays high in its food plant, the majestic incense cedar, flying out to challenge other butterflies that pass by. Fortunately, 'Nelson's' Juniper Hairstreaks often visit flowers, where they can be observed close up.

IDENTIFICATION

Habitat should be enough to separate this subspecies from the other Juniper Hairstreaks. However, the purple scaling on the hindwing below of fresh individuals is diagnostic.

Size: ⅞ to 1 inch

'Nelson's' Juniper Hairstreak

Incense cedar

'Siva' Juniper Hairstreak
Callophrys gryneus siva

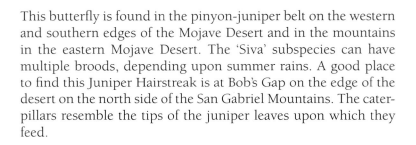

Habitat: Pinyon-juniper areas

Flight Time: March through April, June through July, September through November

Broods: M

Food Plant: California juniper (*Juniperus californica*) and Utah juniper (*Juniperus osteosperma*) in the eastern Mojave Desert

Nectar: Goldenbush (*Isocoma*) and buckwheat (*Eriogonum*)

This butterfly is found in the pinyon-juniper belt on the western and southern edges of the Mojave Desert and in the mountains in the eastern Mojave Desert. The 'Siva' subspecies can have multiple broods, depending upon summer rains. A good place to find this Juniper Hairstreak is at Bob's Gap on the edge of the desert on the north side of the San Gabriel Mountains. The caterpillars resemble the tips of the juniper leaves upon which they feed.

IDENTIFICATION

This subspecies can be confused with the 'Loki' Hairstreak where they come together in the southeastern Mojave, but the 'Siva' has green scaling over much of its hindwing below.

Size: ⅞ to 1⅛ inches

'Siva' Juniper Hairstreak

California juniper

'Loki' Juniper Hairstreak
Callophrys gryneus loki

Habitat: Where California juniper grows at the desert edge

Flight Time: March through April, June through July, September through November

Broods: M

Food Plant: California juniper (*Juniperus californica*)

Nectar: Goldenbush (*Isocoma*) and desert lavender (*Hyptis emoryi*)

This subspecies occurs from the southern Mojave south along the western edge of the Colorado Desert. Like the 'Siva' Hairstreak, the 'Loki' can have multiple broods with summer rains. An excellent place to find this butterfly is Anza-Borrego Desert State Park in areas such as Sentenac Canyon where California juniper grows.

IDENTIFICATION

The 'Loki' looks very much like the 'Thorne's' Juniper Hairstreak (*Callophrys gryneus thornei*), which was just discovered in 1983. The extremely restricted range of the 'Thorne's' is near Otay Mountain in San Diego County, where it feeds on the rare and local Tecate cypress.

Size: 7/8 to 1 inch

Ceraunus Blue female laying eggs on honey mesquite flower head

Ceraunus Blue male

Spring Azure

Celastrina ladon

Habitat: Varied, but shows a preference for wooded areas along streams

Flight Time: February through July

Broods: 2

Food Plant: Wild lilac (*Ceanothus*) flowers and young fruit, dogwood (*Cornus*)

Although this butterfly can be found throughout the lowlands and mountains, it is nowhere common. The best place to find the Spring Azure is along mountain streams, where a number of them will gather at wet sand or mud.

IDENTIFICATION

This species has no strong markings below; in this it is unlike any of our other blues.

Size: ¾ to 1 inch

El Segundo Blue male on food plant

Sea cliff buckwheat

El Segundo Blue male on left, female on right

Arrowhead Blue
Glaucopsyche piasus

Habitat: Forest openings and road cuts
Flight Time: March through June
Broods: 1
Food Plant: Lupine (*Lupinus albifrons* or *L. excubitus*)
Nectar: Buckwheat (*Eriogonum*)

In Southern California, this butterfly is only found in the mountains at higher elevations. A darker coastal race used to be common in the Los Angeles Basin, but it has disappeared with development. The pale arrowhead-shaped markings on its hindwing below give the butterfly its name. This is another species that is ant attended (see page 87). Although never common, the Arrowhead Blue can be regularly found along the Angeles Crest Highway in the San Gabriel Mountains at elevations over 6,000 feet.

IDENTIFICATION

The arrow-shaped marks on the hindwing below are diagnostic. Above, checkered fringes distinguish it from its similar Silvery Blue (*Glaucopsyche lygdamus*) relative.

Size: 1 to 1¼ inches

Arrowhead Blue

Arrowhead Blue female

Silvery Blue
Glaucopsyche lygdamus

Habitat: Many open areas, but especially coastal sage scrub

Flight Time: February through June

Broods: 1

Food Plant: Deerweed (*Lotus scoparius*)

Nectar: Deerweed

In early spring, this large (for a blue), pale blue butterfly can be quite abundant in our lowlands. Later in the spring, it becomes common on the coastal side (cismontane) of our local mountains. Its caterpillars are ant attended (see page 87). The Xerces Blue, a closely related butterfly, became extinct in 1943 when a military facility expanded onto the coastal dunes in the San Francisco area where the last colony resided. That butterfly's name was adopted by the Xerces Society, a worldwide rare insect conservation organization.

IDENTIFICATION

As its name suggests, this butterfly is a silvery blue color and large in comparison to other blues. Below, bold round black spots encircled in white form a postmedian band on the forewing. The black spots on the hindwing are usually smaller, sometimes tiny, and in rare cases nonexistent.

Size: 1 to 1¼ inches

Typical Silvery Blue

Silvery Blue with unspotted hindwing

Palos Verdes Blue
Glaucopsyche lygdamus palosverdesensis

Habitat: Coastal sage scrub
Flight Time: February through April
Broods: 1
Food Plant: California locoweed (*Astragalus trichopodus* var. *lonchus*)

This federally endangered subspecies of the Silvery Blue, which feeds on a particular variety of locoweed, was thought to be extinct when the last known colony was bulldozed in 1983 for a ball field on the Palos Verdes Peninsula in Los Angeles County. The Palos Verdes Blue was rediscovered in 1994 at a Department of Defense oil storage area in nearby San Pedro during a routine insect survey.

IDENTIFICATION

The Palos Verdes Blue is slightly larger than other Silvery Blues.

Size: 1¼ inches

Veined Blue

INSET: *Wright's buckwheat*

Veined Blue

Wright's Metalmark

Mormon Metalmark

Mormon Metalmark

Palmer's Metalmark

Apodemia palmeri

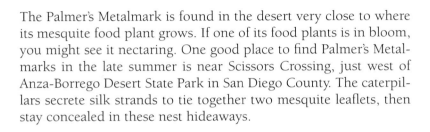

Habitat: Mesquite thickets

Flight Time: April, June through August, October through November

Broods: M

Food Plant: Honey mesquite (*Prosopis glandulosa*)

Nectar: Mesquite flowers and various sunflower family members

The Palmer's Metalmark is found in the desert very close to where its mesquite food plant grows. If one of its food plants is in bloom, you might see it nectaring. One good place to find Palmer's Metalmarks in the late summer is near Scissors Crossing, just west of Anza-Borrego Desert State Park in San Diego County. The caterpillars secrete silk strands to tie together two mesquite leaflets, then stay concealed in these nest hideaways.

IDENTIFICATION

In our area, the Palmer's Metalmark can only be confused with the Mormon Metalmark. However, the Palmer's is paler and grayer overall with an orange edging to the wings that the Mormon lacks.

Size: ¾ to ⅞ inch

Palmer's Metalmark

Honey mesquite

"Brushfoot"

Variable Checkerspot showing "brushfoot"

Johnny-jump-up (violet)

Coronis Fritillary

Coronis Fritillary

Callippe Fritillary
Speyeria callippe

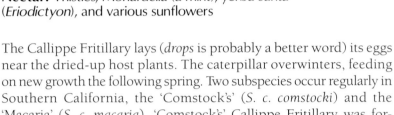

Habitat: Open, grassy foothills and mountain slopes
Flight Time: May through July
Broods: 1
Food Plant: Johnny-jump-up (*Viola pedunculata*)
Nectar: Thistles, *Monardella* (a mint), yerba santa (*Eriodictyon*), and various sunflowers

The Callippe Fritillary lays (*drops* is probably a better word) its eggs near the dried-up host plants. The caterpillar overwinters, feeding on new growth the following spring. Two subspecies occur regularly in Southern California, the 'Comstock's' (*S. c. comstocki*) and the 'Macaria' (*S. c. macaria*). 'Comstock's' Callippe Fritillary was formerly abundant in the foothills of the Los Angeles Basin but is quickly disappearing as development claims its habitat. The 'Macaria' is found from the Mount Piños area east to the northwestern portions of the San Gabriel Mountains.

IDENTIFICATION

The 'Comstock's' subspecies of the Callippe Fritillary, found in the foothills of the Santa Monica, San Gabriel, and Santa Ana Mountains as well as in the local mountains of San Diego County, is brown orange with heavy dark markings above, making it easy to separate from the bright orange and less marked Coronis Fritillary. The 'Macaria' subspecies is much closer in appearance to the Coronis, and the two occur together on Mount Piños and on the northwest side of the San Gabriel Mountains. The 'Macaria' Callippe is a duller orange above, and the marginal silver spots on its hindwing below are more triangular, while those on the Coronis are ovals.

Size: 1⁷/₈ to 2³/₈ inches

'Comstock's' Callippe Fritillary

'Comstock's' Callippe Fritillary

Leanira Checkerspot
Thessalia leanira

Habitat: Mountain foothill chaparral, oak woodlands, desert hills

Flight Time: April through June

Broods: 1

Food Plant: Indian paintbrush (*Castilleja*)

This butterfly occurs in various forms in Southern California. In coastal Santa Barbara and San Luis Obispo Counties, it is mostly black with creamy spots; in the mountains from Los Angeles to San Diego counties it is black, red, and white (see photograph on page 6 in the Introduction); and in the Mojave Desert, it is mainly orange, like the individual in the photograph on the next page. The Leanira Checkerspot may be scarce or absent in our area for many years and then become abundant for a few years. Females lay eggs in masses on the Indian paintbrush food plant, and the caterpillars overwinter in groups.

IDENTIFICATION

Although the Leanira Checkerspot varies above, the hindwing below is distinctive. It is pure white with black lines. All other checkerspots have orange and white banding on their hindwing below.

Size: 1 to 1¾ inches

Variable Checkerspot

INSET: *Variable Checkerspot*

INSET: *Variable Checkerspot desert subspecies* (E.c. corralensis)

Variable Checkerspot dark aberrant

Edith's Checkerspot
Euphydryas editha

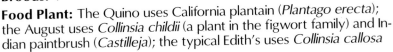

Habitat: Open hills and mesas (*E. e. quino*); yellow pine forest (*E. e. augusta*); mountain foothills and openings (*E. e. editha*)

Flight Time: February through April (*E. e. quino*), May through June (*E. e. augusta*), April through June (*E. e. editha*)

Broods: 1

Food Plant: The Quino uses California plantain (*Plantago erecta*); the August uses *Collinsia childii* (a plant in the figwort family) and Indian paintbrush (*Castilleja*); the typical Edith's uses *Collinsia callosa*

Southern California has three subspecies of the Edith's Checkerspot. One is the endangered Quino Checkerspot (*E. e. quino*), which occurred in Orange, western Riverside, and San Diego Counties away from the immediate coast. It is now probably gone from Orange County and disappearing elsewhere, routed out by development. The second subspecies is the August Checkerspot (*E. e. augusta*), found only in the yellow pine forests of the San Bernardino Mountains. Finally, the typical Edith's (*E. e. editha*), pictured here on the opposite page, just barely gets into the northern part of Southern California in the Piute Mountains. It overwinters as a half-grown caterpillar.

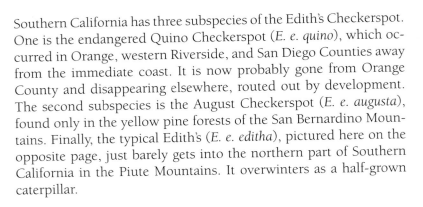

IDENTIFICATION

Some Edith's subspecies can resemble Southern California subspecies of the Variable Checkerspot. However, the Variable's abdomen has white spots along its upper sides, while the Edith's abdomen has no white spots. The Edith's Checkerspot can also be confused with the Leanira Checkerspot, but the Leanira has no orange on the hindwing below.

Size 1⅛ to 1⅞ inches

Edith's Checkerspot

Edith's Checkerspot

Hoary Comma
Polygonia gracilis

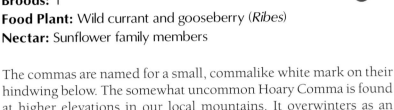

Habitat: Wooded areas at higher elevations
Flight Time: March through September
Broods: 1
Food Plant: Wild currant and gooseberry (*Ribes*)
Nectar: Sunflower family members

The commas are named for a small, commalike white mark on their hindwing below. The somewhat uncommon Hoary Comma is found at higher elevations in our local mountains. It overwinters as an adult, flying in the spring, with the new brood starting to fly in late summer. Unlike many other commas, which mainly feed on sap and rotten fruit as adults, the Hoary Comma primarily nectars on flowers, especially those in the sunflower family. Although this butterfly is quick to dash away when approached, it will usually return to the same perch after a short wait.

IDENTIFICATION

In Southern California, the Hoary Comma can only be confused with the Satyr Comma. However, the Hoary is a darker gray brown below and lacks a hook on its hindwing comma. Above, the Hoary appears to be a two-toned orange with paler margins and has only two black spots in the middle of the hindwing.

Size: 1¾ to 2 inches

California Tortoiseshell

INSET: *Buckbrush*

California Tortoiseshell

Mourning Cloak
Nymphalis antiopa

Habitat: Widespread except in deserts
Flight Time: All year
Broods: M
Food Plant: Willow (*Salix*), cottonwood (*Populus*) and ornamental elms (*Ulmus*)
Nectar: Rotting fruit

Although not common, this beautiful butterfly is regularly seen throughout our region except in the deserts. However, the Mourning Cloak does occur in a few desert canyons where its willow food plant grows. Below, the Mourning Cloak is well camouflaged and looks like tree bark; it can seem to disappear when landing on a tree trunk. The caterpillars feed in groups and can become a pest on ornamental elms. This butterfly is found in Europe; in England it is called the Camberwell Beauty.

IDENTIFICATION

The Mourning Cloak's chocolate brown wings with their creamy yellow margins are unmistakable.

Size: 2⁷⁄₈ to 3³⁄₈ inches

Mourning Cloak
INSET: *Cottonwoods in fall*

INSET: *Willow flowers*
Mourning Cloak

Milbert's Tortoiseshell
Nymphalis milberti

Habitat: Wet meadows
Flight Time: April through September
Broods: 1
Food Plant: Stinging nettle (*Urtica dioica*)

The Milbert's Tortoiseshell is uncommon in Southern California. It lives at higher elevations in open wet meadows where its nettle food plant grows in sunny locations. Its numbers can fluctuate from year to year, but it never has the large-scale emigrations of California Tortoiseshells.

IDENTIFICATION

Except for the much smaller California Patch, no other species resembles this striking butterfly with its wide orange and yellow postmedian band.

Size: 1¾ to 2 inches

Milbert's Tortoiseshell

Milbert's Tortoiseshell

Common Buckeye

Junonia coenia

Habitat: Open areas, especially those that have been disturbed; scarce in deserts

Flight Time: February through November

Broods: M

Food Plant: Most commonly plantain (*Plantago*), but also snapdragon and monkeyflower

The Common Buckeye is fairly common throughout Southern California, except in the desert where it is scarce. It is territorial and will sit on a low perch or on the ground in the middle of a path or a dry wash and fly up to challenge anything that happens by—usually another butterfly, but sometimes a bird or even a butterfly watcher. There is some northward migration in this species in most years.

IDENTIFICATION

The Common Buckeye is an unmistakable butterfly. At first, as it flies up from its low perch in a path or wash and circles around an approaching observer, it looks like a brown blob. After it has assured itself that you are not a female buckeye, it usually returns to the same spot and sits with its wings spread, allowing a good look at its intricate and unique pattern above.

Size: 2 to 2½ inches

Painted Lady

Fiddleneck   *Painted Lady*

West Coast Lady
Vanessa annabella

Habitat: Many and varied

Flight Time: All year

Broods: M

Food Plant: Native and nonnative mallows, especially cheeseweed (*Malva pariviflora*), and nettles (*Urtica*)

Nectar: Thistle and other sunflower family members, yerba santa (*Eriodictyon*), and buckwheat (*Eriogonum*)

Except during large flights of the Painted Lady, the West Coast Lady is the most common of the three ladies in our region. Although you can find the West Coast Lady throughout our region, you will most readily encounter it in urban and suburban habitats where cheeseweed is prevalent.

IDENTIFICATION

Unlike the American and Painted Ladies, the West Coast Lady has an orange bar in the middle of the front edge of the forewing above. The Painted Lady's bar is always white, while the American Lady's can be white, cream, or even pale orange. The West Coast is the only lady with a blue center in each of the four spots on the above hindwing. Below, the five eyespots on the West Coast Lady's hindwing are all the same size and blend into the background. Of the three ladies, the West Coast Lady has the most squared-off wing tips.

Size: 1¾ to 2 inches

West Coast Lady

Checkerbloom (mallow)

West Coast Lady

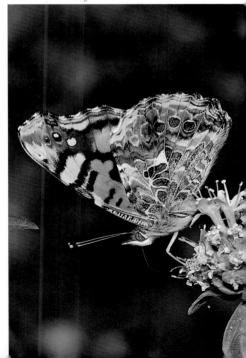

Red Admiral
Vanessa atalanta

Habitat: Many and varied

Flight Time: All year

Broods: M

Food Plant: Nettle family (Urticaceae), including ornamentals such as baby's tears (*Soleirolia soleirolii*)

Nectar: Thistle and other sunflower family members

The Red Admiral can be found throughout our region except in the deserts. It is especially common along streams where its nettle food plant grows. Horse dung and rotting fruit regularly attract this butterfly. It is one of the few butterflies that is regularly seen flying on a sunny day in the dead of winter. A Red Admiral will sometimes pick a particular perch in a backyard and return to it consistently for a few weeks.

IDENTIFICATION

Although the Red Admiral is closely related to the American, Painted, and West Coast Ladies and is in the same genus, it looks different enough that one would rarely mistake it for a lady or any other butterfly. Above, the orange forewing median line and the orange hindwing margin contrast with the black background.

Size: 1¾ to 2¼ inches

Red Admiral

Red Admiral

Baby's tears

Lorquin's Admiral
Limenitis lorquini

Habitat: Along streamsides with willows
Flight Time: April through September
Broods: 2
Food Plant: Willow (*Salix*)

Like many of its admiral relatives, Lorquin's Admiral is territorial. It often perches on the edge of a branch above eye level with its wings half open, ready to chase passing butterflies. It even harasses birds occasionally, a seemingly life-shortening pastime! Young caterpillars are camouflaged by resembling bird droppings. In winter, the caterpillars stay hidden in a rolled-over leaf.

IDENTIFICATION

This species resembles the California Sister in pattern and coloration as well as in flight: they both fly with a few quick flaps and then a glide. One difference is that the orange in the forewing of the Lorquin's Admiral goes out to the wing tips, while the California Sister's orange is more of a spot surrounded by black, and thus never reaches the wing tips. Below, the patterns of the two species are quite different. In addition, unlike the Sister, the Lorquin's Admiral tends to perch with its wings half open.

Size: 2¼ to 2¾ inches

Lorquin's Admiral

Lorquin's Admiral

California Sister
Adelpha bredowii

Habitat: Oak woodlands
Flight Time: March through October
Broods: 2
Food Plant: Oak (*Quercus*)

The California Sister is a common butterfly in our oak woodlands, especially in canyons near streams. It usually stays quite high in the oaks, but does come down to puddle at the edges of streams. On very hot days, California Sisters have been known to land on people to imbibe their salt-filled perspiration. It is said that the name of this butterfly comes from its coloring, which resembles a nun's habit.

IDENTIFICATION

In pattern and coloration, this species resembles the Lorquin's Admiral (see pages 206–7).

Size: 2⁷⁄₈ to 3¹⁄₈ inches

California Sister

California Sister

Common Ringlet
Coenonympha tullia

Habitat: Native grasslands or open oak woodlands
Flight Time: February through September
Broods: M
Food Plant: Bunchgrass (*Festuca*)

The Common Ringlet's off-white color and floppy flight give it the appearance of a moth as it flies low through grassy areas. When it alights, usually low on a blade of grass, it keeps its wings closed. The spring and summer generations of this butterfly differ in color. The spring generation is white above with gray below, while the summer and fall butterflies are cream above with tan below. For many years, authorities considered the 'California' Common Ringlet (*C. t. california*—the subspecies of the Common Ringlet found in Southern California) a separate species. Excellent places to find the Common Ringlet are in the grasslands of Point Mugu State Park's La Jolla Valley on the west end of the Santa Monica Mountains and on the Mission Viejo Land Trust in Orange County.

IDENTIFICATION

The Common Ringlet should not be confused with any other butterfly in Southern California. However, its low, weak flight may cause it to be overlooked as a moth. When it lands, it perches in typical butterfly style with its wings held over its back; then it becomes apparent that it is not a moth.

Size: 1 to 1¾ inches

'California' Common Ringlet, spring form

'California' Common Ringlet, summer form

Great Basin Wood-Nymph

Cercyonis sthenele

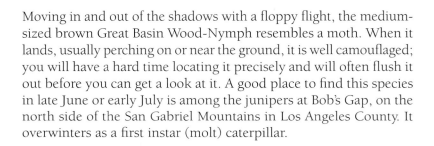

Habitat: Oak savannas, open grasslands in the pinyon pine-juniper belt, or moist canyons in arid country

Flight Time: May through August

Broods: 1

Food Plant: Native bunchgrass (*Festuca*)

Nectar: California buckwheat *(Eriogonum fasciculatum)*

Moving in and out of the shadows with a floppy flight, the medium-sized brown Great Basin Wood-Nymph resembles a moth. When it lands, usually perching on or near the ground, it is well camouflaged; you will have a hard time locating it precisely and will often flush it out before you can get a look at it. A good place to find this species in late June or early July is among the junipers at Bob's Gap, on the north side of the San Gabriel Mountains in Los Angeles County. It overwinters as a first instar (molt) caterpillar.

IDENTIFICATION

In Southern California, there is nothing else quite like this butterfly. Below, the two eyespots on the forewing are sometimes hidden by the hindwing.

Size: 1⅜ to 2 inches

Great Basin Wood-Nymph

MONARCHS *Subfamily Danainae*

Monarch
Danaus plexippus

Habitat: Varied
Flight Time: All year
Broods: M
Food Plant: Milkweed (*Asclepias*)
Nectar: Milkweed and sunflower family members, including mule fat (*Baccharis salicifolia*) and coyote brush (*Baccharis pilularis*)

The Monarch is probably the best-known butterfly in North America because of its well-publicized yearly migration. In spring, the migration begins with the butterflies heading north; butterflies of several generations later return in the fall to their wintering areas. Most Monarchs east of the Rocky Mountains overwinter in the mountains of mainland Mexico, while those from the West usually overwinter on the coast of California and northern Baja California, Mexico. In his book *Chasing Monarchs*, well-known lepidopterist and nature writer Bob Pyle showed that not all western Monarchs stay on the West Coast. He actually followed the flight of some Monarchs from eastern Washington to southeastern Arizona, where he watched them head south across the border into Mexico.

Wintering groups that do stay along the West Coast roost in groves of pine and cypress in Baja; those in Southern California mostly use eucalyptus. In the fall, thousands gather at Big Sycamore Canyon at the western end of the Santa Monica Mountains to roost in sycamores and nectar on mule fat. One of the largest concentrations (tens of thousands of butterflies) winters in a eucalyptus grove just north of Santa Barbara at Ellwood; another large concentration winters near Pismo State Beach's North Beach campground in San Luis Obispo County.

The generation of Monarchs that overwinters lives for about six months. Caterpillars feed on milkweed, which contains toxic chemicals that make adult Monarchs unpalatable to birds. The orange and black aposematic (warning) colors help broadcast this fact.

Queen caterpillar   Queen

Queen

Skippers
Family Hesperiidae

Skippers are different enough from true butterflies to be classified in a separate superfamily. Their name comes from their bouncing, skipping flight. In general, skippers have fatter bodies than true butterflies and are not as colorful, so that they are sometimes mistaken for moths. They do have clubbed antenna, however, which helps distinguish them from most moths. In most skippers, the antennae club has a hook on the end.

Because skippers are usually dark, and because many of them have similar patterns of brown and orange, they present some of the more difficult challenges in butterfly identification. Duskywings in particular remind birders of the identification problems posed by look-alike *Empidonax* flycatchers. Many beginners to butterfly identification find skippers just too difficult. We advise these people to just "skip 'em" at first.

Three subfamilies of skippers occur in California:

- **Spread-wing skippers** (*Pyrginae*) are generally medium sized and perch with their wings spread open.

- **Grass-skippers** (*Hesperiinae*) are usually small, and most feed on grasses—hence the subfamily name. When they land, they hold their wings either closed or open in a unique posture called jet-planing: the hindwings are open and horizontal while the forewings are partially open. This position sometimes confuses novice butterfly watchers as it isn't immediately clear which surfaces are showing. The photograph of the Alkali Skipper opposite illustrates the jet-plane wing position. The left wing surface with the thin black diagonal line is the above forewing, while the unmarked right wing is the above hindwing. The right forewing is almost perpendicular to the viewer and thus is not noticeable. The black line on the

Alkali Skipper male in jet-plane posture

forewing is called the stigma. It is only found on the male of some grass-skippers and consists of raised black scales that produce pheromones.

• **Giant-skippers** (*Megathyminae*) are the largest of our skippers. They feed exclusively on yucca or agave and thus are found mostly in our deserts where these plants are native. The giant-skippers do not have hooks on their antennae clubs.

Many skipper caterpillars pupate in the leaves of their food plant, which they sew together with silk.

Forty-three species of skippers have been found in Southern California.

Silver-Spotted Skipper
Epargyreus clarus

Habitat: Woodland and forest edges or openings
Flight Time: May through September
Broods: 2
Food Plant: Various members of the pea family (Fabaceae)

Unfortunately, this uniquely marked skipper is uncommon in Southern California and is only found in the San Bernardino Mountains. Although it is a spread-wing skipper, it usually perches with the wings held closed, showing off the bright silver spot below that gives the species its name. Even in flight, the silver spots are conspicuous. The caterpillar feeds during the night and hides during the day in a shelter it forms by binding leaf edges together with silk.

IDENTIFICATION

The large size and below hindwing silver spot make this an easy butterfly to identify. A band of irregular orange rectangles on the above forewing is also unique.

Size: 1¾ to 2⅜ inches

Silver-spotted Skipper

Silver-spotted Skipper

Propertius Duskywing
Erynnis propertius

Habitat: Oak woodlands
Flight Time: March through June
Broods: 1
Food Plant: Coast live oak (*Quercus agrifolia*)

Of the six species of duskywings in Southern California, the Propertius is the most distinctive: well-marked gray forewings contrast with brown hindwings. Although its food plant is found throughout our area except in the desert, this butterfly is generally only encountered in the mid-elevations of our local mountains.

IDENTIFICATION

This is the largest of the Southern California duskywings. It has strongly patterned gray forewings and reddish brown hindwings. The Propertius Duskywing has particularly large hyaline (glassy translucent) spots on its forewing that are especially large in the females. The Afranius Duskywing, also found in our local mountains, is similar in color and pattern, but it is darker and much smaller with a more compact shape.

Size: 1¼ to 1¾ inches

Propertius Duskywing male

Two Afranius Duskywings

Mournful Duskywing

Erynnis tristis

Habitat: Oak woodlands

Flight Time: February through September

Broods: M

Food Plant: Coast live oak (*Quercus agrifolia*),
blue oak (*Quercus douglasii*), and valley oak (*Quercus lobata*)

Like the Propertius Duskywing, the Mournful is an oak feeder, but it is more commonly found in the lower elevations of our mountains. The caterpillar makes a protective nest using folded-over oak leaves and later also pupates in this nest.

IDENTIFICATION

This is one of only two duskywings in Southern California with a white trailing edge to the hindwing. The other is the Funereal Duskywing, which looks mostly black, while the Mournful is primarily brown. The hyaline (translucent) spots on the Mournful Duskywing's forewing are usually larger than on the Funereal. This can be confusing, since the female duskywings generally have larger spots than the males, so a male Mournful and a female Funereal may have similar-sized hyaline spots.

Size: 1¼ to 1⅜ inches

Mournful Duskywing

Blue oak

Funereal Duskywing
Erynnis funeralis

Habitat: Varied
Flight Time: February through October
Broods: M
Food Plant: Deerweed (*Lotus scoparius*) and other members of the pea family (Fabaceae)
Nectar: A wide variety including sunflowers, buckwheat (*Eriogonum*), and yerba santa (*Eriodictyon*)

The Funereal Duskywing is the most common and widespread of the duskywings in Southern California, mainly because of the ready availability of its food plants. The males show some territoriality by picking a perch and chasing other butterflies out of the immediate area.

IDENTIFICATION

Because of the white trailing edge to the hindwing, the Funereal Duskywing can only be confused with the Mournful Duskywing in our region. The Funereal is darker—almost black—and has fewer and smaller hyaline (translucent) spots. This is especially true of the males, as female duskywings usually have larger hyaline spots. A key Funereal field mark is the contrasting brown patch in the middle of forewing. If you are in an open area away from oaks it is a good bet that a duskywing with a white edge to the hindwing is a Funereal.

Size: 1⅛ to 1¾ inches

Funereal Duskywing male

Funereal Duskywing female

Common Checkered-Skipper
Pyrgus communis

White Checkered-Skipper
Pyrgus albescens

Habitat: Varied
Flight Time: February through October
Broods: M
Food Plant: Mallow (*Malva* and *Sidalcea*)

Although these two skippers are virtually indistinguishable in the field, they are distinct species with significant differences in the males' genitalia. Whereas the White Checkered-Skipper occurs throughout most of Southern California, the Common Checkered-Skipper just enters our region in northern Kern and San Luis Obispo Counties. These skippers perch on or near the ground.

IDENTIFICATION

In the Laguna Mountains of San Diego County, the somewhat similar-looking Laguna Mountain Skipper (*Pyrgus ruralis lagunae*), a subspecies of the Two-banded Checkered-Skipper, is federally listed as endangered. On this skipper, the bands of white spots in the forewing form an X. The Small Checkered-Skipper, which is encountered sparingly in our deserts, is small, as its name tells us, and has less white above than the White Checkered-Skipper.

Size: ¾ to 1¼ inches

White Checkered-Skipper

White Checkered-Skipper eggs on mallow

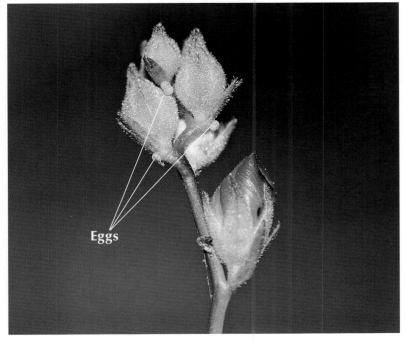

Eggs

Northern White-Skipper
Heliopetes ericetorum

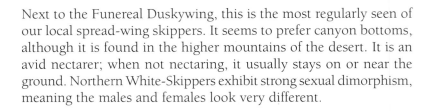

Habitat: Coastal sage scrub and chaparral
Flight Time: March through October
Broods: M
Food Plant: Various mallows (Malvaceae), especially chaparral bush mallow (*Malacothamnus fasciculatus*)
Nectar: Buckwheat (*Eriogonum*), yerba santa (*Eriodictyon*)

Next to the Funereal Duskywing, this is the most regularly seen of our local spread-wing skippers. It seems to prefer canyon bottoms, although it is found in the higher mountains of the desert. It is an avid nectarer; when not nectaring, it usually stays on or near the ground. Northern White-Skippers exhibit strong sexual dimorphism, meaning the males and females look very different.

IDENTIFICATION

The males, which are mostly white above with black chevrons along the wing margins, are unmistakable. At first, a novice butterfly watcher might assume that the Northern White-Skipper is some species of white (Pierinae) butterfly, but the hooked antenna and the fact that it generally perches with its wings open are dead giveaways. The female has more black markings above and might be mistaken for a White Checkered-Skipper, but the wide, white, continuous median band sets the Northern White-Skipper apart. In addition, the Northern White-Skipper is mostly unmarked below, with a couple of pale brown bands on the hindwing, while the White Checkered-Skipper is darker brown with white splotches below with some banding.

Size: 1⅛ to 1⅝ inches

Northern White-Skipper male

Northern White-Skipper female

Orange Skipperling
Copaeodes aurantiacus

Habitat: Arid canyons and washes in the desert
and chaparral on the desert edges
Flight Time: March through October
Broods: M
Food Plant: Grasses (Poaceae)
Nectar: Buckwheat (*Eriogonum*), goldenbush
(*Ericameria*) and other sunflower family members

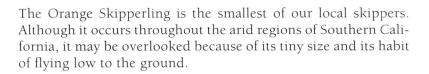

The Orange Skipperling is the smallest of our local skippers.
Although it occurs throughout the arid regions of Southern California, it may be overlooked because of its tiny size and its habit
of flying low to the ground.

IDENTIFICATION

Its small size, orange color, and lack of dark markings
set the Orange Skipperling apart from other butterflies
in Southern California. Some male Alkali Skippers,
uncommon in our local deserts, can be equally small.
However, Alkali Skippers have black borders above
and show a pale ray in the middle of their hindwings
below.

Size: ¾ to ⅞ inch

Orange Skipperling

Orange Skipperling jet-planing (hindwings spread)

Common Branded Skipper

Hesperia comma

Habitat: Varied
Flight Time: May through August
Broods: 1
Food Plant: Grasses (Poaceae)
Nectar: Mint (*Monardella*), buckwheat (*Eriogonum*), and yerba santa (*Eriodictyon*)

Of the grass-skippers inhabiting our local mountains, the Common Branded Skipper is usually the most common. This species is widely distributed in the West and has much geographic variation.

IDENTIFICATION

The best way to identify this species is to see the hindwing below. Although a number of local skippers, such as Juba, Columbian, and Lindsey's, have white or pale contrasting markings on the hindwing below, the key to identifying the Common Branded is the pale marking closest to the body that resembles a "C".

Size: ⁷⁄₈ to 1 inch

Common Branded Skipper

Juba Skipper

Fiery Skipper
Hylephila phyleus

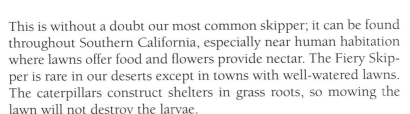

Habitat: Anywhere with lawns
Flight Time: All year
Broods: M
Food Plant: Grasses (Poaceae), including crab grass
Nectar: Many, including, lantana, sunflower family members, and fog fruit (*Lippia*)

This is without a doubt our most common skipper; it can be found throughout Southern California, especially near human habitation where lawns offer food and flowers provide nectar. The Fiery Skipper is rare in our deserts except in towns with well-watered lawns. The caterpillars construct shelters in grass roots, so mowing the lawn will not destroy the larvae.

IDENTIFICATION

If you are going to learn to identify grass-skippers, this abundant butterfly is the one to start with and to get to know thoroughly. The male is a fiery orange above with jagged black borders. The photograph of the male shows it holding its wings in the typical jet-plane posture. The wing on the right with some black spots in the center is the forewing, while the wing on the left is the hindwing. The left forewing is almost perpendicular to the camera in the photo and is thus hard to distinguish. The female is duller orange and has more dark markings above. Below, both the male and the female have a number of small dots on the hindwing that are diagnostic for this species. The noticeably shorter antennae are also useful in distinguishing the Fiery Skipper from other orange skippers.

Size: 1 to 1¼ inches

Fiery Skipper female jet-planing

Fiery Skipper male jet-planing (hindwing left, forewing right)

Fiery Skipper male

Sandhill Skipper
Polites sabuleti

Habitat: Drier grasslands, but lawns as well
Flight Time: April through September
Broods: M
Food Plant: Saltgrass (*Distichlis spicata*)
Nectar: Wild heliotrope (*Heliotropium curassavicum*)

This butterfly's food plant is adapted to a sandy environment and can tolerate salt or alkali, so it usually grows near the immediate coast or in the desert. The Sandhill Skipper normally occurs in both of these two widely separated areas. The coastal butterflies are considered a different subspecies from those in the desert. The Sandhill Skipper prefers staying close to the ground and can be found nectaring on low-growing flowers like wild heliotrope.

IDENTIFICATION

Below, the complex pattern on the hindwing, which is difficult to describe, is unique. The desert subspecies has a similar but paler hindwing. Above, the male's stigma mark (raised black scales that produce pheromones) in the middle of the forewing forms an "S". It is difficult to make this out in the photograph because the stigma is superimposed on a large black spot.

Size: ¾ to 1⅛ inches

Sandhill Skipper male

Sandhill Skipper male

Eufala Skipper
Lerodea eufala

Habitat: Open areas in coastal lowlands and desert valleys

Flight Time: June through November

Broods: 2

Food Plant: Grasses (Poaceae)

Nectar: Lantana

Without a doubt, this is our most bland-looking skipper. It is found only in our lowlands, both along the coast and in the desert, and doesn't appear until the heat of summer arrives.

IDENTIFICATION

Below, the plain gray brown hindwing is like no other local skipper. The forewing above has a series of three to five hyaline (translucent) spots in the middle of the wing. The uncommon Wandering Skipper that occurs around some of our local coastal river mouths is also plain, but it has two pale spots on the hindwing below.

Size: ⁷/₈ to 1¼ inches

Eufala Skipper

Eufala Skipper

Woodland Skipper
Ochlodes sylvanoides

Habitat: Many, including coastal sage scrub, chaparral, and oak woodlands
Flight Time: June through October
Broods: 1
Food Plant: Grasses (Poaceae), including rye grass
Nectar: Everlasting (*Gnaphalium*)

In late summer and early fall, this skipper can be abundant in native habitats from near the coast to the middle elevations of our local mountains.

IDENTIFICATION

The Woodland Skipper's hindwing below can vary from an unmarked orange brown (as in the photo) to pale blocky markings. Above, the male is mostly orange with uneven dark margins and a long, heavy stigma (raised black scales that produce pheromones) in the middle of the forewing. The stigma connects to the dark markings on the margins at the wing apex. The female has the same general pattern, but is duller and has no stigma. The similar Rural Skipper flies earlier, is slightly smaller, and has one or more hyaline (translucent) spots near the forewing tips.

Size: ¾ to 1⅛ inches

Woodland Skipper male jet-planing

Woodland Skipper

Rural Skipper
Ochlodes agricola

Habitat: Forest and woodland openings, especially near streams or road cuts

Flight Time: April through July

Broods: 1

Food Plant: Grasses (Poaceae)

This is a common skipper throughout native habitats in the spring and early summer.

IDENTIFICATION

Except for the Orange Skipperling, the Rural Skipper is the smallest of our local skippers. It resembles the later-flying Woodland Skipper, but can be distinguished from this and other orange and brown grass-skippers by the hyaline (translucent) spots near the forewing tips.

Size: ¾ to 1 inch

Rural Skipper female

Rural Skipper male jet-planing

Umber Skipper
Poanes melane

Habitat: Wet places, lawns
Flight Time: January through November
Broods: 2
Food Plant: Grasses (Poaceae)

The common Umber Skipper is equally at home on a well-watered lawn or at a streamside opening in the forest. It is the largest of the regularly occurring grass-skippers in Southern California.

IDENTIFICATION

The large size, chestnut color below, and series of large orange (males) or cream-colored (females) spots in the middle of the forewing above make this skipper distinctive.

Size: 1⅛ to 1⅜ inches

Umber Skipper

Umber Skipper

GIANT-SKIPPERS *Subfamily Megathyminae*

California Giant-Skipper
Agathymus stephensi

Habitat: Along the western edge of the Colorado Desert where its food plant grows
Flight Time: September through October
Broods: 1
Food Plant: Desert agave (*Agave deserti*)

The giant-skippers are in their own subfamily. True to their name, they are large skippers with fat bodies. They are found mostly in our deserts, feeding on agaves and yuccas. Agave feeders, such as the California Giant-Skipper, fly in the fall and yucca (including Joshua tree) feeders fly in the spring. Giant-skippers are usually hard to find and even harder to see, since they zip about quite rapidly. They don't nectar much, but will occasionally come to water. The California Giant-Skipper can best be observed at the southern end of Anza-Borrego Desert State Park, especially in the late afternoon as it comes back to roost on or near the food plant. The caterpillars burrow into the fleshy agave leaves and build a trapdoor on the leaf underside just before they pupate. The famous "worm" in bottles of mescal (an alcoholic beverage made from agaves) is not a worm, but is in fact the caterpillar of a giant-skipper.

IDENTIFICATION

This is the only giant-skipper that flies in the fall on the western edge of the Colorado Desert. The Yucca Giant-Skipper, found in the same area, only flies in early spring and is much darker.

Size: 2 to 2⅛ inches

California Giant-Skipper on desert agave leaf

Desert agave flower head

Desert agave (century plant)

Yucca Giant-Skipper
Megathymus yuccae

Habitat: Along the western and southern edges of the Mojave Desert as well as in its eastern mountains, and on the western edge of the Colorado Desert where its food plant grows

Flight Time: March through April

Broods: 1

Food Plant: Joshua tree (*Yucca brevifolia*), Mojave yucca (*Yucca schidigera*), banana yucca (*Yucca baccata*)

This spring-flying species is the most widespread of our giant-skippers and can be found all the way across the country to Florida wherever its yucca food plant is native. The western subspecies, including three in Southern California, were formerly considered a separate species (*M. coloradensis*). There is one disjoint population in Del Mar, San Diego County. The females lay their eggs on young shoots of yuccas, and newly hatched caterpillars chew their way into the center of the plant. There they construct a silk shelter attached to the core leaves. The adults don't seem to nectar and are rarely seen.

IDENTIFICATION

This is the only giant-skipper in Southern California that flies in the spring. Its larger size and almost black undersides make it unmistakable. The gray edges of the hindwing curve over the body when it perches.

Size: 2 to 2⅛ inches

Yucca Giant-Skipper

Mojave yucca

Greenish Blue

Southern California Butterfly Checklist

SWALLOWTAILS Family Papilionidae

☐ Pipevine Swallowtail — *Battus philenor*
☐ **'Desert' Black Swallowtail** — ***Papilio polyxenes coloro***
☐ 'Baird's' Old World Swallowtail — *Papilio machaon bairdii*
☐ **Anise Swallowtail** — ***Papilio zelicaon***
☐ Indra Swallowtail — *Papilio indra*
☐ **Giant Swallowtail** — ***Papilio cresphontes***
☐ **Western Tiger Swallowtail** — ***Papilio rutulus***
☐ Two-tailed Swallowtail* — *Papilio multicaudata*
☐ **Pale Swallowtail** — ***Papilio eurymedon***

WHITES AND SULPHURS Family Pieridae

Whites *Subfamily Pierinae*

☐ Pine White* — *Neophasia menapia*
☐ **Becker's White** — ***Pontia beckerii***
☐ Spring White* — *Pontia sisymbrii*
☐ **Checkered White** — ***Pontia protodice***
☐ **Cabbage White** — ***Pieris rapae***
☐ Pearly Marble — *Euchloe hyantis*
   ☐ 'California' Pearly Marble — *E. h. hyantis*
   ☐ 'Desert' Pearly Marble — *E. h. lotta*
☐ Desert Orangetip — *Anthocharis cethura*
☐ **Sara Orangetip** — ***Anthocharis sara***
   ☐ **'Pacific' Sara Orangetip** — ***A. s. sara***
   ☐ 'Thoosa' Sara Orangetip — *A. s. thoosa*
☐ Gray Marble — *Anthocharis lanceolata*

Sulphurs *Subfamily Coliadinae*

☐ Clouded Sulphur — *Colias philodice*
☐ **Orange Sulphur** — ***Colias eurytheme***
☐ Queen Alexandra's Sulphur (Harford's) — *Colias alexandra harfordii*
☐ **California Dogface** — ***Colias eurydice***
☐ Southern Dogface* — *Colias cesonia*
☐ **Cloudless Sulphur** — ***Phoebis sennae***

☐ Large Orange Sulphur*	*Phoebis agarithe*
☐ Mexican Yellow*	*Eurema mexicana*
☐ **Sleepy Orange**	***Eurema nicippe***
☐ **Dainty Sulphur**	*Nathalis iole*

GOSSAMER-WING BUTTERFLIES Family Lycaenidae

Coppers *Subfamily Lycaeninae*

☐ **Tailed Copper**	***Lycaena arota***
☐ Great Copper	*Lycaena xanthoides*
☐ **Gorgon Copper**	***Lycaena gorgon***
☐ Blue Copper*	*Lycaena heteronea*
☐ Purplish Copper	*Lycaena helloides*
☐ **Hermes Copper**	***Lycaena hermes***

Hairstreaks *Subfamily Theclinae*

☐ **Golden Hairstreak**	***Habrodais grunus***
☐ **Great Purple Hairstreak**	***Atlides halesus***
☐ Silver-banded Hairstreak	*Chlorostrymon simaethis*
☐ **Behr's Hairstreak**	***Satyrium behrii***
☐ **California Hairstreak**	***Satyrium californica***
☐ Sylvan Hairstreak*	*Satyrium sylvinus*
☐ Gold-hunter's Hairstreak*	*Satyrium auretorum*
☐ **Mountain Mahogany Hairstreak**	***Satyrium tetra***
☐ **Hedgerow Hairstreak**	***Satyrium saepium***
☐ **Bramble Hairstreak**	***Callophrys dumetorum***
☐ Sheridan's Hairstreak	*Callophrys sheridanii*
☐ **Brown Elfin**	***Callophrys augustinus***
☐ Desert Elfin	*Callophrys fotis*
☐ Moss' Elfin	*Callophrys mossii*
☐ **Western Pine Elfin**	***Callophrys eryphon***
☐ Thicket Hairstreak	*Callophrys spinetorum*
☐ **Juniper Hairstreak**	***Callophrys gryneus***
☐ 'Siva' Juniper Hairstreak	*C. g. siva*
☐ 'Nelson's' Juniper Hairstreak	*C. g. nelsoni*
☐ 'Loki' Juniper Hairstreak	*C. g. loki*
☐ 'Thorne's' Juniper Hairstreak*	*C. g. thornei*
☐ **Gray Hairstreak**	***Strymon melinus***
☐ Avalon Scrub-Hairstreak	*Strymon avalona*
☐ Mallow Scrub-Hairstreak	*Strymon istapa*
☐ Leda Ministreak	*Ministrymon leda*

Blues *Subfamily Polyommatinae*

☐ **Western Pygmy Blue**	***Brephidium exile***
☐ **Marine Blue**	***Leptotes marina***
☐ **Ceraunus Blue**	***Hemiargus ceraunus***
☐ Reakirt's Blue	*Hemiargus isola*

☐ Western Tailed-Blue	*Everes amyntula*
☐ Spring Azure	*Celastrina ladon*
☐ Sonoran Blue	*Philotes sonorensis*
☐ Square-spotted Blue	*Euphilotes battoides*
☐ 'Bernardino' Square-spotted Blue	*E. b. bernardino*
☐ El Segundo Blue‡	*E. b. allyni*
☐ 'Ellis' Square-spotted Blue	*E. b. ellisi*
☐ Dotted Blue	*Euphilotes enoptes*
☐ 'Pacific' Dotted Blue	*E. e. enoptes*
☐ 'Mojave' Dotted Blue	*E. e. mojave*
☐ 'Dammer's' Dotted Blue	*E. e. dammersi*
☐ Rita Blue	*Euphilotes rita*
☐ Small Blue	*Philotiella speciosa*
☐ **Arrowhead Blue**	***Glaucopsyche piasus***
☐ **Silvery Blue**	***Glaucopsyche lygdamus***
☐ **Palos Verdes Blue‡**	***G. l. palosverdesensis***
☐ **Melissa Blue**	***Lycaeides melissa***
☐ Greenish Blue*	*Plebejus saepiolus*
☐ **San Emigdio Blue**	***Plebejus emigdionis***
☐ **Boisduval's Blue**	***Plebejus icarioides***
☐ **Acmon Blue**	***Plebejus acmon***
☐ **Lupine Blue**	***Plebejus lupinus***
☐ **Veined Blue**	***Plebejus neurona***

METALMARKS   Family Riodinidae

☐ **Fatal Metalmark**	***Calephelis nemesis***
☐ Wright's Metalmark*	*Calephelis wrighti*
☐ **Mormon Metalmark**	***Apodemia mormo***
☐ **Palmer's Metalmark**	***Apodemia palmeri***

BRUSHFOOTED BUTTERFLIES   Family Nymphalidae

Snouts   ***Subfamily Libytheinae***

☐ American Snout*	*Libytheana carinenta*

Heliconians and Fritillaries   ***Subfamily Heliconiinae***

☐ **Gulf Fritillary**	***Agraulis vanillae***
☐ Variegated Fritillary	*Euptoieta claudia*
☐ **Coronis Fritillary**	***Speyeria coronis***
☐ Unsilvered Fritillary	*Speyeria adiaste*
☐ **Callippe Fritillary**	***Speyeria callippe***
☐ Great Basin Fritillary	*Speyeria egleis*
☐ Hydaspe Fritillary	*Speyeria hydaspe*
☐ Pacific Fritillary	*Boloria epithore*

True Brushfoots   *Subfamily Nymphalinae*

- [ ] **Leanira Checkerspot** — *Thessalia leanira*
- [ ] **California Patch** — *Chlosyne californica*
- [ ] **Bordered Patch** — *Chlosyne lacinia*
- [ ] Northern Checkerspot — *Chlosyne palla*
- [ ] Sagebrush Checkerspot — *Chlosyne acastus*
- [ ] **Gabb's Checkerspot** — *Chlosyne gabbii*
- [ ] **Tiny Checkerspot** — *Dymasia dymas*
- [ ] Phaon Crescent — *Phyciodes phaon*
- [ ] Pearl Crescent — *Phyciodes tharos*
- [ ] **Mylitta Crescent** — *Phyciodes mylitta*
- [ ] **Variable Checkerspot** — *Euphydryas chalcedona*
- [ ] **Edith's Checkerspot** — *Euphydryas editha*
  - [ ] Quino Checkerspot‡ — *E. e. quino*
- [ ] **Satyr Comma** — *Polygonia satyrus*
- [ ] **Hoary Comma** — *Polygonia gracilis*
- [ ] **California Tortoiseshell** — *Nymphalis californica*
- [ ] **Mourning Cloak** — *Nymphalis antiopa*
- [ ] **Milbert's Tortoiseshell** — *Nymphalis milberti*
- [ ] **American Lady** — *Vanessa virginiensis*
- [ ] **Painted Lady** — *Vanessa cardui*
- [ ] **West Coast Lady** — *Vanessa annabella*
- [ ] **Red Admiral** — *Vanessa atalanta*
- [ ] **Common Buckeye** — *Junonia coenia*
- [ ] Tropical Buckeye — *Junonia genoveva*

Admirals and Relatives   *Subfamily Limenitidinae*

- [ ] Viceroy — *Limenitis archippus*
- [ ] **Lorquin's Admiral** — *Limenitis lorquini*
- [ ] **California Sister** — *Adelpha bredowii*

Satyrs   *Subfamily Satyrinae*

- [ ] **Common Ringlet** — *Coenonympha tullia*
- [ ] **Great Basin Wood-Nymph** — *Cercyonis sthenele*

Monarchs   *Subfamily Danainae*

- [ ] **Monarch** — *Danaus plexippus*
- [ ] **Queen** — *Danaus gilippus*

SKIPPERS   Family Hesperiidae

Spread-Wing Skippers   *Subfamily Pyrginae*

- [ ] **Silver-spotted Skipper** — *Epargyreus clarus*
- [ ] Hammock Skipper — *Polygonus leo*
- [ ] Northern Cloudywing — *Thorybes pylades*
- [ ] Golden-headed Scallopwing — *Staphylus ceos*
- [ ] Arizona powered-Skipper — *Systasea zampa*
- [ ] Sleepy Duskywing — *Erynnis brizo*

☐ **Propertius Duskywing**	*Erynnis propertius*
☐ **Mournful Duskywing**	*Erynnis tristis*
☐ Pacuvius Duskywing	*Erynnis pacuvius*
☐ **Funereal Duskywing**	*Erynnis funeralis*
☐ Afranius Duskywing*	*Erynnis afranius*
☐ Two-banded Checkered-Skipper	*Pyrgus ruralis*
☐ Laguna Mountain Skipper‡	*P. r. lagunae*
☐ Small Checkered-Skipper	*Pyrgus scriptura*
☐ **Common Checkered-Skipper**	*Pyrgus communis*
☐ **White Checkered-Skipper**	*Pyrgus albescens*
☐ Erichson's White-Skipper	*Heliopetes domicella*
☐ **Northern White-Skipper**	*Heliopetes ericetorum*
☐ Common Sootywing	*Pholisora catullus*
☐ Mojave Sootywing	*Hesperopsis libya*
☐ Saltbush Sootywing*	*Hesperopsis alpheus*

Grass-Skippers   Subfamily Hesperiinae

☐ Julia's Skipper	*Nastra julia*
☐ **Orange Skipperling**	*Copaeodes aurantiaca*
☐ **Fiery Skipper**	*Hylephila phyleus*
☐ Alkali Skipper*	*Pseudocopaeodes eunus*
☐ Juba Skipper*	*Hesperia juba*
☐ **Common Branded Skipper**	*Hesperia comma*
☐ Pahaska Skipper	*Hesperia pahaska*
☐ Columbian Skipper	*Hesperia columbia*
☐ Lindsey's Skipper	*Hesperia lindseyi*
☐ Carus Skipper	*Polites carus*
☐ **Sandhill Skipper**	*Polites sabuleti*
☐ Sonoran Skipper	*Polites sonora*
☐ Sachem	*Atalopedes campestris*
☐ **Woodland Skipper**	*Ochlodes sylvanoides*
☐ **Rural Skipper**	*Ochlodes agricola*
☐ **Umber Skipper**	*Poanes melane*
☐ Dun Skipper	*Euphyes vestris*
☐ **Eufala Skipper**	*Lerodea eufala*
☐ Brazilian Skipper	*Calpodes ethlius*
☐ Wandering Skipper	*Panoquina errans*

Giant-Skippers   Subfamily Megathyminae

☐ Arizona Giant-Skipper	*Agathymus aryxna*
☐ **California Giant-Skipper**	*Agathymus stephensi*
☐ Mojave Giant-Skipper	*Agathymus alliae*
☐ **Yucca Giant-Skipper**	*Megathymus yuccae*

Butterflies in **bold** have a full write-up and photograph in this book
*Butterfly has photograph only in this book
‡Butterfly is federally listed as Endangered Species

SUGGESTED RESOURCES

Books and Publications

Identification and Distribution

Brock, Jim P., and Kenn Kaufman. *Butterflies of North America* (Kaufman Focus Guide). Boston: Houghton Mifflin, 2003.
Very easy to use; photos of live butterflies are digitally manipulated to enhance field marks.

Butterflies of North America. U.S. Geological Survey, Northern Prairie Wildlife Center: www.npwrc.usgs.gov/resource/distr/lepid/bflyusa/bflyusa.htm
Butterfly maps and lists to county level, photographs, and species information.

Dameron, Wanda. *Searching for Butterflies in Southern California*. Los Angeles: Flutterby Press, 1997.
Best places and times to find each species; various area lists make butterfly trip planning more productive. Descriptions and line drawings of caterpillar food plants. Contact Flutterby Press at 23424 Jonathan Street, Los Angeles, CA 91304. Phone: (818) 340-0365.

Emmel, Thomas C., and John F. Emmel. *The Butterflies of Southern California*. Los Angeles: Natural History Museum of Los Angeles County, 1973.
Excellent information on distribution of Southern California butterflies. Ten color plates show pinned specimens (some images rather small) of all the Southern California butterfly species and subspecies.

Garth, John S., and J. W. Tilden. Illustrated by David Mooney. *California Butterflies*. Berkeley: University of California Press, 1986.
Good California butterfly distribution information. Plates are paintings of specimens.

Glassberg, Jeffrey. *Butterflies through Binoculars: The West: A Field Guide to the Butterflies of Western North America.* Oxford: Oxford University Press, 2001.

The best butterfly field identification guide in the West, with photographs of living butterflies in natural settings.

Mattoni, Rudi. *Butterflies of Greater Los Angeles.* Beverly Hills: Lepidopterist Research Foundation, 1990; Reissued 2001.

Excellent color photos of specimens of all Los Angeles Basin butterflies—those found below 2,500 feet elevation. Brief but complete information on flight times, habitat, food plants, etc. in neatly folded poster-size format.

Opler, Paul. Illustrated by Amy Bartlett Wright. *A Field Guide to Western Butterflies* (The Peterson Field Guide Series). Boston: Houghton Mifflin, 1999.

Good text, although some names and taxonomy are unique to this book. Illustrations are paintings of butterflies in living poses; the details on the smaller butterflies do not shown up well.

Pyle, Robert Michael. *National Audubon Society Field Guide to North American Butterflies.* New York: Alfred A. Knopf, 1981.

Excellent text, illustrated with good photographs of live butterflies. Large area of coverage means subspecies shown may not look like those seen locally.

Watching

Pyle, Robert Michael. *Handbook for Butterfly Watchers.* Boston: Houghton Mifflin, 1988.

A beautifully written and fascinating look at butterflies and how to enjoy watching them. Excellent for the novice and seasoned watcher alike.

Gardening

Donahue, Julian P. *Butterfly Gardening in Southern California.* Los Angeles: Natural History Museum of Los Angeles County, 1999.

An excellent little booklet covering our local butterflies.

Tekulsky, Mathew. *The Butterfly Garden: Turning Your Garden, Window Box, or Backyard into a Beautiful Home for Butterflies.* Boston: Harvard Common Press, 1985.

The Xerces Society. *Butterfly Gardening: Creating Summer Magic in Your Garden.* San Francisco: Sierra Club Books, 1998.

Plants

Hickman, James C., ed. *The Jepson Manual: Higher Plants of California.* Berkeley: University of California Press, 1993.
> *An authoritative and comprehensive identification guide to the almost 8,000 plants that grow wild in California, illustrated with 4,000 line drawings.*

Associations

North American Butterfly Association (NABA)
4 Delaware Road
Morristown, NJ 07960
(973) 285-0907
www.naba.org
Butterfly information, recent sightings, local chapter contact information.

Lepidopterists' Society
http://alpha.furman.edu/~snyder/snyder/lep/
International organization with a focus on butterflies and moths. Brings together professional scientists and amateur enthusiasts to study and enjoy the Lepidoptera.

Lorquin Entomological Society
www.nhm.org/research/entomology/LorquinSoc/

Xerces Society
4828 Hawthorne Blvd.
Portland, OR 97215
(503) 232-6639
www.xerces.org

Southern California Natural History Museums

Entomology Research Museum
University of California, Riverside
(909)787-5294
http://www.cnas.ucr.edu/cnas//facilities/entresmus.html
Research collections and public displays.

Natural History Museum of Los Angeles County

Los Angeles
(213) 763-DINO
www.nhm.org
Has had summertime enclosed outdoor butterfly exhibit with free-flying live butterflies. Appointments required to examine collections. Also serves as meeting place for Lorquin Entomological Society (www.nhm.org/research/entomology/LorquinSoc/).

Orange County Natural History Museum

Laguna Niguel
(949) 831-3287
www.ocnha.mus.ca.us

Palm Springs Desert Museum

Palm Springs
(760) 325-7186
www.psmuseum.org

San Bernardino County Museum

Redlands
(909) 307-2669
www.co.san-bernardino.ca.us/museum

San Diego Natural History Museum

San Diego
(619) 232-3821
www.sdnhm.org
Had live Monarch exhibit. Appointments required to examine collections.

Santa Barbara Museum of Natural History

Santa Barbara
(805) 682-4711
www.sbnature.org

Places to Watch Butterflies
in Southern California

The following spots are good places to find butterflies in season (see Introduction pages 25 to 35). Many have visitor centers and bookstores that can provide specialized local information.

State Parks
www.cal-parks.ca.gov

The following Southern California state parks provide a great diversity of natural habitats.

Antelope Valley California Poppy State Reserve
Los Angeles County

Anza-Borrego Desert State Park
San Diego County
The best Colorado Desert and desert edge butterfly spot, especially in March or after summer or early fall rains.

Chino Hills State Park
Orange County
Good riparian and grassland habitat.

Malibu Creek State Park
Los Angeles County
Excellent springtime and early summer spot for riparian and coastal sage scrub butterflies.

Montaña de Oro State Park
San Luis Obispo County

Mount San Jacinto State Park
Riverside County
High mountain meadow species in summer. Accessed by tram from Palm Springs.

Palomar Mountain State Park
San Diego County
Excellent spring and summer area especially for mountain meadow species.

Pismo State Beach
San Luis Obispo County
One of the largest U.S. Monarch overwintering sites is in a eucalyptus grove just south of the North Beach Campground. Oso Flaco Lake and

the Guadalupe-Nipomo Dunes, owned by The Nature Consevancy, are just south (see http://www.tnccalifornia.com/our_proj/guadalupe/visit.asp).

Placerita Canyon State and County Park
Los Angeles County
Nice riparian habitat surrounded by oak woodlands.

Point Mugu State Park
Ventura County
Sycamore and La Jolla Canyons are excellent for coastal sage scrub and riparian species in early spring. Sycamore Canyon is a fall gathering area for Monarchs.

Red Rock Canyon State Park
Kern County
An excellent scenic spot to find Mojave Desert species in early spring.

Topanga State Park
Los Angeles County

Torrey Pines State Beach and State Reserve
San Diego County

National Forests

In Southern California, national forests cover much of our local mountains, making them good places to seek out butterflies in the summer.

Angeles National Forest
Los Angeles County
www.r5.fs.fed.us/angeles/
In summer, look along the roadsides such Angeles Crest and Angeles Forest Highways. San Gabriel Canyon and Mount Baldy areas are also good in summer.

Cleveland National Forest
Orange, Riverside, and San Diego Counties
www.r5.fs.fed.us/cleveland/
Trabuco and Silverado Canyons in the Santa Ana Mountains, Palomar Mountain, and the meadows of the Laguna Mountains are good summer spots.

Los Padres National Forest

San Luis Obispo, Santa Barbara, Kern, and Ventura Counties
www.r5.fs.fed.us/lospadres/
The Mount Piños area is a particularly good place to access high moun-
tain and mountain meadow butterflies.

San Bernardino National Forest

San Bernardino and Riverside Counties
www.r5.fs.fed.us/sanbernardino/
Areas such as Barton Flats, Baldwin Lake, Onyx Summit, Sugarloaf
Mountain, and Bluff Meadow in the San Bernardino Mountains are ex-
cellent for various species throughout the summer.

National Parks, Preserves, Refuges, and Recreation Areas

Although we only have a handful of national preserves in Southern
California, each is a natural treasure to be enjoyed over and over.

Channel Islands National Park

www.nps.gov/chis/
Park islands have good diversity, including unique subspecies. Santa
Catalina, although not part of the national park, does have the endemic
Avalon Hairstreak.

Joshua Tree National Park

www.nps.gov/jotr/
A great place to find both Mojave (for example, at Indian Cove in the
north) and Colorado (at Cottonwood Spring in the south) Desert species.

Mojave National Preserve

www.nps.gov/moja/
Has many Mojave Desert species that aren't found elsewhere in Southern
California. Good in spring and after summer rains.

Salton Sea National Wildlife Refuge

http://pacific.fws.gov/salton/
Colorado Desert species.

Santa Monica Mountains National Recreational Area

www.nps.gov/samo/
Best in spring, especially areas that are within the state parks (see State
Parks, above).

Gardens and Zoos

Because our local gardens and zoos are landscaped with many flowers, you can find a fair number of butterflies in these locations.

Descanso Gardens
La Cañada
(818) 949-4200
www.descanso.com

Huntington Library, Art Collections, and Botanical Gardens
San Marino
(626) 405-2100
www.huntington.org

Living Desert Zoo and Gardens
Palm Desert
(760) 346-5694
www.livingdesert.org

Los Angeles County Botanic Garden
Arcadia
(626) 821-3222
www.arboretum.org

Los Angeles Zoo
Los Angeles
(323) 662-6400
www.lazoo.org

Rancho Santa Ana Botanic Garden
Claremont
(909) 625-8767
www.rsabg.org/

San Diego Wild Animal Park
Escondido (760) 747-8702
www.sandiegozoo.org
Has indoor exhibit with living, free-flying butterflies from all over the world.

San Diego Zoo
San Diego
(619)234-3135
www.sandiegozoo.org

Santa Barbara Botanic Garden
Santa Barbara
(805) 682-4726
www.santabarbarabotanicgarden.org

South Coast Botanic Garden
Palos Verdes Peninsula
(310) 544-6815
www.parks.co.la.ca.us/south_coast_botanic.html

Wrigley Memorial and Gardens
Avalon, Santa Catalina Island
(310) 510-2595
www.catalina.com/memorial.html

Other Areas

Charmlee Wilderness Park
Malibu
www.coastalconservancy.ca.gov/Wheel/lapage/1_malibu/charm.html
Coastal sage scrub and oak woodlands with small museum. Excellent in early spring.

Huntington Central Park
Huntington Beach
www.fsnc.org/
Many Gulf Fritillaries in various life cycle stages inhabit the passionvine around the Shipley Nature Center.

Mission Trails Regional Park
San Diego
www.mtrp.org
Excellent area for Hermes Copper and Queen.

Mojave Narrows Regional Park
Victorville
www.co.san-bernardino.ca.us/parks/mojave.htm
Desert riparian species.

Monrovia Canyon Park
Monrovia
www.ci.monrovia.ca.us/city_hall/public_works/canyon_park/canyon_park.htm
Excellent California Dogface spot. An annual NABA butterfly count happens here.

O'Neill Regional Park
Mission Viejo
www.ocparks.com/oneillpark/
Good for open grassland species such as Common Ringlet and Callippe Fritillary.

Santa Rosa Plateau Ecological Preserve
www.santarosaplateau.org/
Excellent grassland and open oak woodland habitat.

Upper Newport Bay Regional Park
Newport Beach
www.ocparks.com/uppernewportbay/
Salt marsh edge that is the best spot in Southern California for Wandering Skipper.

BUTTERFLY INDEX

FOOD PLANT INDEX

telegraph weed, 176, 177
Thamnosma montana, 56
thistle, 180, 181, 200
turpentine broom, 56, 57

Ulmus, 192
Urtica, 200, 202
   dioica, 188, 194
Urticaceae, 204

vetch, 76
Viguiera parishii, 172
Viola pedunculata, 166, 168

whitethorn, 65
wild currant, 88, 186
wild licorice, 142
wild lilac, 64, 100, 104, 108, 126, 190
wild radish, 72
willow, 62, 192, 193, 206

yucca
   banana, 252
   Mojave, 252, 253
Yucca
   baccata, 252
   brevifolia, 252
   schidigera, 252